The Broken God

The Broken God
Power under Control

David E. Schroeder

Baker Books

A Division of Baker Book House Co
Grand Rapids, Michigan 49516

Published by Baker Books
a division of Baker Book House Company
P.O. Box 6287, Grand Rapids, MI 49516-6287

Printed in the United States of America

Library of Congress Cataloging-in-Publication Data

Schroeder, David E.
    The broken God : power under control / David E. Schroeder.
       p.   cm.
    Includes bibliographical references.
    ISBN 0-8010-8376-1
    1. Jesus Christ—Passion—Meditations. I. Title.
BT431.S32 1994
232.96—dc20   94-3498

Contents

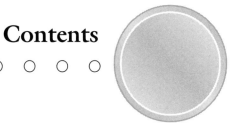

Preface

Books on the passion of Jesus fertilize the soul. They energize devotion and refresh the spirit. They set the communion table and transport us into the Holy of Holies. They play the chords of worship and convey us through history's most meaningful three days to leave us adoring at his feet.

Whether you are a new believer looking for assurance, whether you are in the doldrums of spiritual depression, whether you are seeking to add vitality to Lent, Jesus' passion is the perfect elixir for your soul. Whether you read classics like Krummacher's *The Suffering Saviour*, and Denney's *The Death of Christ*, or enjoy more contemporary books like Lucado's *No Wonder They Call Him the Savior*, you are sure to be greatly blessed. Even books featuring an apologetic approach, such as Frank Morrison's *Who Moved the Stone?* will greatly stimulate your faith.

Just as Jesus exhorted his disciples to continue to remember him through frequent reenactments of the Last Supper, so as Christians today we are in need of fresh statements about our Lord's passion. This book will not be superior to those books cited above, just as one communion service does not seek to be superior and diminish the value of others. *The Broken God* is a fresh statement, a new partaking with diverse elements. In these pages you will find much devotional reflection—these words were not written without tears.

You will also find exhortation; the events of our Lord's passion were not inspired by God's Spirit merely to fill in our gaps of historical knowledge. An apologetic flavor also seasons these chapters in the same spirit as that of the evangelist John when he wrote, "that you may believe."

What events in that last week leading up to the crucifixion are actually to be considered part of our Lord's passion? The first three chapters of *The Broken God* discuss events that are considered to be prepassion: the anointing, the Last Supper, and the garden prayer. Jesus certainly suffered during these events, but the anguish was internal and not yet physical. The remaining chapters take us from the arrest in the garden, through two trials, to the crucifixion, burial, and finally, the resurrection.

As I studied the events of our Lord's passion, his embodiment of the eight beatitudes in the eight events that led up to the resurrection became very obvious. The structure of this book is an overlay of the beatitudes on the episodes of the passion of Jesus. If he could continue to demonstrate such grace and character under the most extreme stress imaginable, there is hope for us.

Jesus opened his public ministry with the Sermon on the Mount, recorded most fully in Matthew 5–7. The introduction of the sermon consists of eight pithy statements, which we call the Beatitudes. They are formulas that may be applied to our lives if we are willing to pay for the extra blessing by accepting the sacrifice required. It's sort of like getting better seats at the stadium if you are willing to pay a higher ticket price.

The Beatitudes are fundamental and imperative to Christian living. If the Sermon on the Mount can be considered the constitution of the kingdom of God, the Beatitudes form the preamble, the heavenly bill of rights, so to speak. If we expect to live here and hereafter in the presence of royalty, the King of Kings, we need to know fitting behavior. The Beatitudes provide that palace protocol. They do not tell us how to be happy, but how to *be;* as a by-product of these attitudes we are blessed.

Unlike the Jewish religious leaders of his day, Jesus did not tell his followers how they should live and then model an entirely different lifestyle. Jesus lived the Beatitudes consistently. Sometimes we hear admonitions to live a Christlike life. We wonder what that means. We need look no farther than the Beatitudes—they are the essence of Christ's life. In each episode of his life, we can see at least one of the eight Beatitudes shining through. And that is the point of this book—to demonstrate that, even in the midst of the most traumatic week any human has ever experienced, Jesus faithfully demonstrated these gracious character qualities. He did so living from the inside out. That is to say, Jesus was not forcing himself through heroic discipline to act contrary to his character. Rather, because he lived God-centered, Jesus was just being himself.

We can be greatly encouraged by his model. Life at the end of the second millennium is very stressful. The post-industrial information age, with all its high-tech gadgets that supposedly simplify life, threatens every day to cause us to crack. The word *stress* originally was an engineering term that referred to the amount of weight and pressure a particular beam or structure could support. Now it is used most frequently as a psychological term.

Books on coping have proliferated in the past few decades, a sure indication of our society's preoccupation with stress. This is not such a book. We are not concerned here with coping, but with character. The answer to today's stress is not in psychological gimmickry, but in spiritual character. The subtitle of this book, *Power under Control*, suggests a special way to respond to stress—the way Jesus handled it. Rather than exploding or imploding, Jesus effectively reversed the energy of stress by passive power. As we gain greater character transformation and learn to live the Beatitudes, that passive power will enable us to respond better to the pressures in our lives. And not only will this be best for us, the people around us will also benefit from the blessing.

If you plan to use this book with a group, the group study questions at the end of the chapters provide an outstanding framework for devotional exercises during the weeks of Lent. The questions are also suitable for individual study at any time of the year.

Besides hoping that this book will be a blessing to the general Christian public, I have written it with a more specific group in mind. In the last decade of this millennium a significant men's movement has emerged. Unlike the much celebrated feminist movement beginning in the 1970s, the men's movement is more subdued and somber. The feminist movement is about rights; the men's movement is about responsibility. There is little celebration or triumphalism as men are seeing that many of the social and spiritual ills of our nation are due to poor fathering and inadequate modeling of character.

Sensing a great need among men, I started an organization called MasterWorks in 1986, the result of which has been the formation of many small groups throughout the nation that meet weekly to consider what it means to be a Christian man in today's society. My book, *"Follow Me": The Master's Plan for Men,* supplemented by *The "Follow Me" Manual,* is widely used to help men understand and conform to Jesus' expectations for a disciple.

One of the chief tenets of *"Follow Me"* is that in regard to discipleship, Jesus always emphasized character transformation; he never focused on outer disciplines and seldom discussed ministry skills. He began discipleship lessons with "be-attitudes," not "do-activities." The beatitudes are eight pithy sayings that not only encompass the qualities Jesus himself embodied but also define a truly godly person. If today's men try, like some of those first-century men, to develop these eight character qualities, children, wives, churches, communities, nations, and the world will indeed be blessed.

Event	Beatitude Jesus Displayed
The Anointing	Peacemakers
The Last Supper	Hunger and Thirst for Righteousness
The Garden Prayer	Mourn
The Arrest	Merciful
The Jewish Trial	Pure in Heart
The Roman Trial	Meek
The Crucifixion	Persecuted because of Righteousness
The Burial	Poor in Spirit
The Resurrection	Blessed

In my eagerness to see men be transformed, I offer *The Broken God* as a sequel to *"Follow Me": The Master's Plan for Men.* My great joy will be to hear that MasterWorks groups have moved from the first text to this one, which describes not only the ultimate passion but also the ultimate pattern of Christlike living.

The Anointing

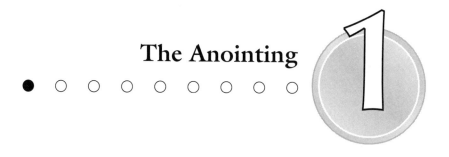

Mark 14:1–11

"Leave her alone," said Jesus.
"Why are you bothering her?
She has done a beautiful thing to me."
Mark 14:6 NIV

Blessed are the peacemakers.

Is there one week that you can recall as being truly life changing? History has had such a week—a week that changed everything! No other week—from the flood in Noah's time to the nuclear bombing of Japan in World War II—was as pivotal to history as the Passion Week.

The exact sequence of events in Passion Week is not clear. For example, Jesus' anointing by Mary occurred perhaps in Simon the Leper's home, which was likely Jesus' lodging place most of the nights of Holy Week. Thus, on which particular evening this event may have occurred is only conjecture.

We do know that prior to the anointing, Jesus had experienced an extremely stressful day because he had been confronted by various antagonistic parties. Mark 11 tells about Jesus' wonderful triumphal entry into Jerusalem in which he was largely hailed as a messianic figure. Unknowingly, the people, hungering for the fulfillment of the Lord's promises to Israel, were stoking the flames of indignation of the Jewish leaders who already had plotted to kill Jesus.

Dangerous Dialogue

On this particular day, Jesus was first confronted by chief priests, scribes, and elders who challenged his authority in cleansing the temple from its money changers (Mark 11:27). Jesus responded to their challenge by spotlighting their sinister motives, putting them in exactly the same bind of their having to answer a self-condemning question. He asked, "Was the baptism of John from heaven, or from men?" (Mark 11:30). These leaders knew that if, on the one hand, they admitted that John's baptism was from heaven, Jesus would counter by asking why they did not then believe him. On the other hand, if they admitted what they really believed, that John's baptism was merely a human convention, they were afraid of being branded as heretics because many believed that John was a fresh, God-given, prophetic voice. Therefore in their cowardice they answered that they did not know. Jesus answered them by saying, "Neither will I tell you by what authority I do these things" (v. 33). This is what he implied: Just as you have a conviction about John the Baptist and are unwilling to state it, so I know the source of my authority but am unwilling to state it to you.

This confrontation was soon followed by another from the antipathetic Pharisees and Herodians, the Pharisees being strict separatists from Roman influence, and the Herodians being fully comfortable with the Roman enculturation of Judea. Their questions to Jesus focused on the legitimacy of paying tax to Rome. The Pharisees, of course, expected him to say that it was not legitimate for an orthodox Jew to give tax to Caesar, while the Herodians held the contrary position. Jesus' response shut them up, and ever since has been a wonderful guideline for Christian believers regarding both God

> *He asked Jesus an age-old question,*
> *which all Jews loved to debate,*
> *"What commandment is the foremost of all?"*

and society: "Render to Caesar the things that are Caesar's, and to God the things that are God's" (Mark 12:17).

The third confrontation came from Sadducees, a more liberal Jewish sect that doubted the reality of resurrection. They spawned an interesting story about a woman who survived seven husbands who were brothers and who, according to Jewish practice, were required to marry the widow. The question then was, "In the resurrection, when they rise again, which one's wife will she be?" (Mark 12:23). Their attempt to make Jesus appear foolish rebounded in their faces more rapidly than it was sent. Jesus told them how mistaken they were because they did not understand the Scriptures nor the power of God. The resurrection life will not include marriage, for people will be similar to angels in heaven. He went on to give them a lesson regarding resurrection from a book of Moses, part of the Scriptures in which they did profess belief.

The last challenge came from a scribe who seemed legitimately impressed with Jesus' wisdom. He asked Jesus an age-old question, which all Jews loved to debate, "What commandment is the foremost of all?" (Mark 12:28). Jesus gave him a twofold answer: Love the Lord with all your heart, soul, mind, and strength and, second in importance, love your neighbor as yourself.

Jesus' arduous day continued as he taught in the temple regarding his messiahship as the son of David. While in the temple, Jesus and the disciples were watching people put money into the treasury. Jesus, observing a poor widow putting in two small copper coins, commented on how great an offering she was presenting—greater than all of the other contributors because she gave out of her poverty while they gave out of their abundance.

As Jesus and his disciples were leaving Jerusalem and heading east across the Kidron Valley toward Bethany, the disciples, looking back on the majesty of the temple, commented on its grandeur. This discussion elicited the eschatological discourse of our Lord Jesus found in Mark 13, Matthew 24, and Luke 21.[1]

An Unusual Anointing

This brings us to the holy of holies of Mark's Gospel, chapters 14–16, which begins with a story that has warmed the hearts of Christians for centuries. Indeed Jesus prophesied in the midst of this story that the event itself would be proclaimed in the whole world through time immemorial because of the precious devotion rendered to him. As we ask what this story contributes to the account of the passion of Jesus, we are impressed by the interesting contrast it presents of people's attitudes toward Jesus as he approached his death.

From the accounts in Matthew 26:6–13, John 12:1–8, and Mark 14:1–11, we are able to piece the story together. On one of the week nights early in Holy Week, our Lord was in the home of Simon the Leper, perhaps being honored in an open feast at which many from the immediate community were guests. About Simon the Leper, little is known. Obviously, being present, he was no longer a leper; otherwise, he would be banished from the community. Some speculate that Jesus had healed him. Some suggest that while this was the house of Simon the Leper, Simon himself may not have been there, either having already died, or perhaps being yet in a leper community. Others suggest that Simon was either the father or the deceased husband of Martha. These latter two ideas bear some credibility as we see how comfortable Mary, Martha, and Lazarus seem to be in this home.

We are told that the crowd was there not only to honor Jesus but also because of fascination with Lazarus, who had been dead for four days and had been resurrected by Jesus. In fact, the fame of this incident had so covered the territory of Judea that the Jewish leaders were seeking a way to put Lazarus to death to stop the rumor. During the feasting, Mary of Bethany, the sister of Lazarus and Martha, approached Jesus carrying a family heirloom, an alabaster vial of very expensive perfume. While it would not be unusual to pour a few drops of this fragrance on the head of an important guest, Mary very lavishly poured the entire contents on Jesus, anointing first his head and then his feet.

> *To be a peacemaker is to put one's own well-being, reputation, and life on the line to be a reconciler.*

Some of the disciples, apparently led by Judas Iscariot, protested the wasting of the expensive perfume, which the Gospel writers tell us was worth nearly a whole year's wages. The pretext for the complaint was that the money might have been contributed to the poor. Jesus, who normally had the greatest compassion for the poor, rebuked their scolding of Mary and affirmed her for having done a good deed to him. The poor, he said, would always be with them and they could at any time do good to the poor. He, on the other hand, would not always be with them. Mary had greater insight into his coming death, and Jesus interpreted her loving act as a preburial anointing. Then, in a yet greater act of affirmation, Jesus said that wherever the gospel would be preached in the whole world, Mary's passionate act of devotion would be told in memory of her.

The Gospel writers go on to tell us that Judas Iscariot then left the band of disciples and went off to the chief priests to betray Jesus.

Blessed Are the Peacemakers

Here we see peacemaking at its best. Some assume that peacemaking always involves compromise, and sometimes it does. More often compromise is more necessary for peacekeeping than for peacemaking. Jesus did not commend peacekeeping but peacemaking. What's the difference?

Those who try to keep peace often confuse means and ends by thinking peace itself is the goal even if truth, honor, and justice must be compromised. For Jesus, peace is a by-product that often accompanies right living, but it should not be an end in itself. Peace at any price is not a biblical concept. Had Jesus been concerned only about keeping peace, he could not have made peace between mankind and God.

To be a peacemaker is to put one's own well-being, reputation, and life on the line to be a reconciler. The peacemaker is far more concerned about whole relationships than with the petty issues that divide brothers. Rivalry, competitiveness, social distinctions, and self-advancement are abhorrent to the peacemaker who views God's family holistically.

In this incident in Bethany, honor required Jesus to take a stand. Mary's deed was rightly motivated; the disciples' rebuke was not. Rather than trying to effect a compromise by pointing out the right and wrong of each side, Jesus the peacemaker confronted the disciples, corrected their understanding, and fully affirmed Mary. Did this tactic make peace? Apparently so—the disciples were the ones who honored Mary by reporting this event.

Being a peacemaker requires courage. Some might think peacemakers are soft, cowardly wimps who can't handle conflict. Far from it! Stepping between two hostile parties takes a strong constitution, especially when it demands taking one side against the other. No wonder those who emulate our Lord's peacemaking "shall be called sons of God" (Matt. 5:9).

Responses to Jesus

We said earlier that this story is included for its value in portraying various human responses toward Jesus as he approached death, and in the story we see four interesting responses. There were the obvious opponents, a complex traitor, loyal but insensitive followers, and a devoted love.

The Obvious Opponents

There were those who were clearly declared opponents. Mark mentions that the chief priests and scribes were seeking how to seize Jesus secretly and kill him (14:1–2). They had agreed not to do it during the festival when the population of Jerusalem was greatly swelled and included many from Galilee who would be ardent followers of Jesus.

We must ask why the religious leaders were so violently opposed to Jesus. Think of the tragedy here. Those who were trusted with the most important elements of the nation, its values and spiritual destiny, were the ones most violently opposed to the Messiah. Mark records three prior occasions when the chief priests and scribes were eager to kill Jesus: after Jesus healed the man's withered hand (3:1–6), after he cleansed the temple (11:15–18), and after they were offended by Jesus' authority (12:1–12).

What was it about Jesus that engendered such hostility? One suggestion is that his personal power and charisma greatly threatened them. Think of his interaction with them as he was about to heal a paralyzed man by saying, "Your sins are forgiven you" (Luke 5:20). Their indignation over his brash pronouncement deserved his well-stated reply, "Which is easier, to say, 'Your sins have been forgiven you' or to say, 'Rise and walk'?" (5:23). Clearly Jesus possessed a power that went beyond position or title. The authority of his teaching and his words literally transformed people.

A second factor that engendered their hostility was his direct, one-to-one relationship with God and his refusal to observe all the traditions that the elders heaped on people. His experiential theology was something quite unique in Judea at the time. The heavy veil that hung in the temple, separating the Holy Place from the Holy of Holies, subtly symbolized the huge veil of religion that separated the people of Israel from a true personal, experiential knowledge of God.

A third factor that engendered their hostility was that the Jewish leaders certainly did not believe God would choose such a humble, irreligious Messiah—someone who defied their conventions and did not endorse their brand of Judaism.

Thus, the Jewish leaders' intention to murder Jesus was almost a frenzied feeding on their insecurity and blind prejudice. They had two problems, however. The first was timing. It was two days before Passover, the biggest religious festival in Jerusalem.[2] The second problem was that Jesus was a very popular figure, as evidenced by his triumphal entry (now celebrated as Palm Sunday). Particularly adoring of Jesus were many who traveled from Galilee, having heard his gracious teachings and witnessed many of his miracles.

Who are Jesus' declared opponents today? Dare we say that they are people who hold many of the same values as those early Jewish leaders? They are people who won't accept the messiahship of Jesus. Many of them are religious leaders who pervert the truth, who hold a closed worldview, and who do not believe God may act unconventionally (supernaturally) in his own world. They are those who accept Jesus only on their own terms, trying to fit him into their own philosophy or their own religion. Some have suggested that the adoring, cheering crowds of Palm Sunday were the same ones yelling, "Crucify him; crucify him!" on that fateful Good Friday. Hailing a Messiah as a champion in a parade is far different than believing in him even while he is being led to execution. Likewise, we

> ### *In many ways the secret enemies of Jesus are more dangerous than the avowed enemies of Jesus.*

are eager to embrace religious truth that affirms our more deeply held convictions about the realities of life than we are to allow truth to transform our own views.

A Complex Traitor

A second response to Jesus is that of a secret enemy—Judas Iscariot. Up to this point Judas had been trusted by the disciples. Later they found he had been a thief all along, but even during the Last Supper, when Jesus mentioned that one of them would betray him, the other eleven did not suspect Judas more than any of the others.

What was Judas's motive? Many books have been written about this interesting man. Perhaps what we do not know about him is more significant than what we do know. Was his motive strictly a desire for money, seen in his weakly veiled protest over Mary's extravagant and apparently wasteful act? Surely he was not concerned about the poor, and John implies strongly that Judas had intended all along to profit from selling the ointment.

Perhaps he was disillusioned with Jesus. By Jesus' referring to the anointing not as a coronation but an anointing for burial, Judas may have thought, "Well, that's it. My last hope is gone. Jesus refuses his rightful kingship."

A third possibility is that Judas was a zealot who wanted Jesus to take power against the Roman government. His agenda did not include the spiritual goals of messiahship that Jesus embraced, but the political deliverance of the nation of Israel.

Whatever his motives, Judas collaborated with Jesus' avowed enemies and was determined to deliver him for a price. In many ways the secret enemies of Jesus are more dangerous than the avowed enemies of Jesus. Who are these secret enemies today? Well, if they are parallel to the first-century secret enemies, they are found within the ranks of the followers—those who are discontented; those who have an "I love Jesus, but . . ." mentality; those who have been greatly discouraged by an unfulfilled expectation. They are those who have priorities other than love and loyalty to Jesus— priorities of financial gain or reputation. They are idealists who live for the wrong ideal.

Nearly every pastor can cite at least one story of a church member into whose life came some great disappointment. That person had the opportunity either to reaffirm confidence in God's plan and care or to allow that great disappointment to strangle faith, proclaiming God to be unworthy of trust. Such people often go on to become avowed enemies of Jesus after a time of secret disbelief.

Other secret enemies misunderstand Jesus' identity and have false expectations of him. Some of them are doctrinal deviants. They deny his deity and his uniqueness. They see him simply as a religious symbol and example. Ultimately they forsake the Christian community just as Judas did.

Loyal but Insensitive Followers

Next are Jesus' practical followers. Here we see the disciples. They were loyal. They had learned well the lessons Jesus taught, including the lesson of charity and concern for the poor. Like other believers, however, they allowed their practicality to override their spiritual passion. It did not matter that the expensive ointment and the flask were not theirs. Like so many of us, they were good at knowing how other people should use their money. They saw an abuse of funds and cried foul. They were right in every other way but insensitive to the moment, and became indignant.

Often, practical followers are those who are very loyal. But loyalty does not equal love. Jesus' followers called the anointing a waste, even though the perfume was used on the Christ, their master, the Son of God. One social commentator has observed that the number one cause of family fighting is money. Likely this is true in the church as well. The church can truly be too extravagant in its use of funds, but it cannot be too extravagant for Christ. One of the important questions faced by churches today is how much money should be spent on buildings. In medieval days, communities built extravagant cathedrals as monuments to their worship of God. Today, those who lavishly use funds in such ways are likely to be condemned by those who believe that since a church is not a building, funds should not be wasted on construction. Rent a hall, they say, or buy an inexpensive prefab building, but reserve the money for more spiritual goals.

We do not have a definitive answer for this ongoing issue. Mary's extravagance certainly was not practical, but it was right at that particular moment. We must be careful before strongly condemning the way others choose to express their love for Christ.

Practical followers today are, for the most part, loyal servants of Christ. But many have lost their first love, and religion has become more important than relationship. Sensitivity to God's agenda has been lost.

A Devoted Love

Finally, we see his devoted lovers, expressed most clearly through the life of Mary. Mary's act truly was an expression of devoted love. Anointing normally symbolized one of three things. Sometimes it was a prophetic act for a mission, such as the anointing of a king. Samuel anointed young David as a symbol that he would one day be king. In 2 Kings 9 Jehu was anointed to be king of Israel. Was Mary motivated by this idea? T. W. Manson suggests that Mary's anointing may have been intended as a coronation, which Jesus then turned into the idea of anointing for burial.[3]

Anointing was also known to be an act performed by a prostitute. Luke 7:36–39 tells a story, similar to the story of Mary in Mark 14, of a woman, a sinner who, while Jesus was dining in the home of a Pharisee, entered with an alabaster vial of perfume. In the spirit of repentance, after wetting Jesus' feet with her tears and wiping them with her hair, she anointed them with the perfume. Obviously

> *Sometimes we do the right thing*
> *at the wrong time. Jesus commended Mary*
> *because she anointed him beforehand.*

we are not suggesting here that she was doing this as part of her trade. The use of an ointment like this was perhaps the only extravagant way she had for expressing her love for Jesus.

The most common purpose for anointing people was for burial, an act that was done usually by women. The particular ointment used was an aromatic oil extracted from a root native to India. We have already seen that its value was equal to a year's wages for a working man. The ointment was contained in an alabaster flask, which was likely a family heirloom passed down through generations from mother to daughter. Mark adds to our understanding of the extravagance of Mary's act by saying that she broke the vial after pouring all the ointment on Jesus' head. The significance of breaking the flask was as a sign that all the ointment was used. Mary was not trying to retain any of the perfume.

What a beautiful symbol of the need for believers to be fully broken so that God can use every part of us. Perhaps this was the picture the apostle Paul had in mind in 2 Corinthians 2:14–16 (NIV):

> But thanks be to God, who always leads us in triumphal procession in Christ and through us spreads everywhere the fragrance of the knowledge of him. For we are to God the aroma of Christ among those who are being saved and those who are perishing. To the one we are the smell of death; to the other, the fragrance of life.

Furthermore Mary's breaking the flask was a tribute to the greatness of Jesus. When a distinguished guest came—a person so great one might meet him or her only once—the oil flask would be broken so that it could never be used again. This is similar to a modern day sports practice of retiring the jersey number of a very, very great player. As tribute to that player's extremely unusual and valuable contribution, his number would never again be used by that team. Mary's breaking the flask also symbolized her understanding of Jesus' upcoming burial, for after a body was anointed for burial, the pieces of the flask were often placed in the tomb with the body.

A Beautiful Thing

The response of Jesus to the disciples after they began criticizing Mary is well known. The Revised Standard Version says, "She has done a beautiful thing to me" (Mark 14:6). Why was this act so beautiful? A first observation is that true love is always sacrificial and not calculating. First Chronicles 11 relates a wonderful story of a similar act of great sacrificial love. During the heat of a strenuous battle, David longed for water from a well in enemy-held territory. Three of his men, hearing this, and with total disregard for their own safety, broke through the enemy line, went to the well, gathered water, returned through the enemy line, and carried the water to David as an expression of their great devotion to him. Recognizing this great act of self-sacrifice and devotion, David responded not by thanking them and drinking the water but by pouring the water out before the Lord saying, "Be it far from me before my God that I should do this. Shall I drink the blood of these men who went at the risk of their lives? For at the risk of their lives they brought it" (1 Chron. 11:19).

Secondly, Mary's act was beautiful because true love *acts* on the impulse of love. A well-known saying in our day is, "The road to hell is paved with good intentions." Many of us talk about our love for Jesus, but few find ways to express it. Mary was able to act on her love, and her act was extremely appropriate. Sometimes we offer love that is not what the loved one really needs. Mary, unlike the others, seemed to understand what was going on in the life of Jesus. Perhaps she was the only one who took seriously his prediction that he would suffer at the hands of the chief priests, scribes, and elders and be handed over to the Gentiles to be murdered.

Her love was also expressed in a most timely manner. Sometimes we do the right thing at the wrong time. Jesus commended Mary because she anointed him *beforehand* in preparation for his burial. Often the greatest acts of love have only one moment for expression—a birthday, an anniversary, a word of congratulations, a word of comfort. Often the timing of an act of love will confuse other people. Normally God places a high priority on caring for the poor, but this particular moment was the right time for Mary's expression of love. Furthermore, her act was beautiful because of its intensity. She was extravagant in her love because the situation called for extravagance. So, Mary was commended for acting on the impulse of her love.

Thirdly, true love is not self-conscious. Mary was totally impervious to potential criticism for wasting expensive ointment and breaking a valuable flask. Within seconds the fragrant aroma of the ointment filled the room, indicating to everyone that something unusual was occurring. Mary cared little that others might criticize her. Often true love must be expressed despite the potential criticism from others. In fact, when we take time to worry about the response of others to an act of love that we intend to do, perhaps we have already lost the edge of that love.

Mary gave great honor through her devotion, but think what she received in return. Instead of breaking a flask, Jesus allowed his body to be broken for her. Instead of sacrificing an ointment, Jesus allowed his blood to be sacrificed to God. As we consider the Passion Week of our Lord Jesus, a few heroic figures emerge, but the most tender act of love and devotion, the boldest expression of courage, the most compassionate response to the plight of Jesus all pale compared with the radical, unreasonable love of our Lord for our souls.

Mary ministered to Jesus prior to his death; Jesus went to his death so he might win eternal life for Mary and millions more. As the peacemaker, Jesus brought harmony not only to the home in Bethany but also between humans and God, not by compromise, but by sacrifice—his own shed blood.

Before putting aside this passage you should ask yourself: What is the flask of ointment in my life that would best express my love for Jesus? What extravagant act of love would be a blessing to him? After pondering that thought, make a commitment to the Lord and at the appropriate time break the flask.

Group Study

Read Mark 14:1–11 and John 12:1–11.

1. What new information do you find in Matthew 26:6–16?
2. Luke 7:36–38 tells a similar story. In response to a Pharisee's indignation, Jesus told a parable (verses 40–47). What

additional insights about extravagant love are suggested in this parable?

3. John's account of this story refers twice to Lazarus. Why was he significant in this event?

4. Mary's motive and Jesus' explanation may have as background an understanding of Psalm 41 and Deuteronomy 15:7–11. What important parallels do you find?

5. Who really objected to the "waste" of perfume? Why did the Gospel writers not identify him at this point?

6. This little story is filled with emotion and conflict. Try to identify the various feelings and relationships in the story.

7. What would you understand to be the difference between peacekeeping and peacemaking? Which do you see most in Jesus?

8. What qualities are necessary for one to be a peacemaker? What is the special promise for peacemakers (Matt. 5:9)?

9. Mary's act was an expression of radical, uncalculating love. What examples from Scripture or your own life are similar?

10. Why would Mary's act be remembered perpetually (Mark 14:9)? What does it have to do with preaching the gospel?

11. What acts of devotion toward Jesus might be a fragrance that fills the house (see John 12:3)?

12. Do you see yourself in the story? With whom do you most readily identify?

The Last Supper

○ ● ○ ○ ○ ○ ○ ○ ○

Mark 14:12–31

**This is my blood of the covenant, which is poured out
for many for the forgiveness of sins.**
Matthew 26:28 NIV

**Blessed are those who hunger and thirst
for righteousness.**

Eating is a mysterious activity. We take physical material into our inner organs that act together like a factory to process the fuel and turn most of it into energy. Material food sustains life and gives energy.

Eating, therefore, is a good analogy for spiritual life. In John 6:48–51, Jesus said,

I am the bread of life. Your fathers ate the manna in the wilderness, and they died. This is the bread which comes down out of heaven, so that one may eat of it and not die. I am the living bread that came down out of heaven; if anyone eats of this bread, he shall live for-

25

ever; and the bread also which I shall give for the life of the world is
My flesh.

If physical eating is somewhat mysterious, these verses point to an
even greater mystery—how we can partake of Jesus and turn that
into spiritual life.

> ### No truth is more important to understand
> ### than the doctrine of the substitutionary atonement.

During Jesus' earthly life there were very few things that he did for
personal comfort, satisfaction, or enjoyment. He was always serv-
ing others. But just before this doubly significant dinner, the Passover
celebration and the institution of the Lord's Supper, Jesus said, "I
have earnestly desired to eat this Passover with you before I suffer"
(Luke 22:15).

Why this intense eagerness? What was there about this Passover
that gave Jesus such a deep yearning? The significance of the Passover
could be traced back nearly fifteen hundred years to the exodus
when the Passover was first celebrated. There is a crucial link between
the Passover celebration and the passion of Jesus. Type and antitype
come together in these two events, and Jesus wanted to make sure
his disciples understood. No truth is more important to understand
than the doctrine of the substitutionary atonement. This doctrine
is best understood by looking closely at the Last Supper.

Typology is a special kind of biblical interpretation that finds a
correspondence between a person, event, or object in the Old Testament and a person, event, or object in the New Testament. For
example, in 1 Peter 3:20–21 the apostle states that the flood of
Noah, through which faithful people were delivered, corresponds
to Christian baptism—type and antitype. A cautionary word is in
order. Some Bible students are easily swept into fanciful biblical
interpretation and invent their own types and antitypes. We are on
much safer ground when we allow the Scriptures to indicate to us
when there is such a correspondence.

Jesus was most eager for his disciples to see that the Jewish ritual of sacrificing a lamb (type) to atone for sins was God's preparation for the sacrifice of the One Lamb of God (antitype) for the sins of the world. He wanted them to see that the Passover meal was but a type of the meal they were about to eat. Later he indicated that even the Last Supper was a type of yet another meal, the great banquet of the Messiah after his second coming. Jesus' eagerness for the disciples to understand the fulfillment of the Passover is well expressed in his statement, "I have earnestly desired to eat this Passover *[pascha]* with you before I suffer *[pathein]*" (Luke 22:15). The root word for both *Passover* and *suffer* is the basis for our word, *passion*. When we speak about the passion of our Lord Jesus, we are talking about his suffering. He was most eager for his followers to understand his suffering in the light of the Passover, which had enabled the Jewish people to be delivered (saved) out of their dire situation. That this message was communicated that night cannot be doubted.

Blessed Are Those Who Hunger and Thirst for Righteousness

Jesus desired to observe this Passover with his disciples for another reason. This meal would symbolize a big step in God's plan of redemption; his way of winning righteousness for his people. Clearly, this was a moment when Jesus demonstrated that he hungered and thirsted for righteousness. He yearned to share the meal that would symbolize how his body and blood would satisfy justice and win righteousness before God.

To hunger and thirst for righteousness may be interpreted as having powerful cravings that are theological (as in justification), moral (as in personal behavior), and social (as in civil justice). In the beatitudes social justice seemed to be Jesus' primary concern. His people are those who seek humanity's liberation from sin's oppression; who promote civil rights; and who work for justice in the law courts, integrity in business dealings, and honor in home and family affairs.

Social justice without theological justice (righteousness and justice are the same word in Greek) is inadequate. Jesus did not come merely to reconcile people to people, but people to God. The righteousness of God is the dominant theme of Paul's letter to the Romans. Paul gloried in the gospel because in it God's righteousness is revealed. Thus, the righteousness of God is best defined as God's righteous way of putting people right with himself by bestowing his righteousness on them.

This beatitude promises that those who hunger and thirst for righteousness will be filled. Certainly Jesus did not mean we should hunger and thirst for our own righteousness, because almost immediately after the Beatitudes he said to the disciples, "Unless your righteousness surpasses that of the scribes and Pharisees, you shall not enter the kingdom of heaven" (Matt. 5:20). Truly we need to hunger and thirst for God's righteousness.

Jesus hungered for righteousness to be accomplished; we hunger for it to be applied.

The Passover

Looking more closely at the text we see in verses 12–16 the careful preparation for the Passover slaughter. The background of this festival meal is found in Exodus 12. Israel was in bondage in Egypt. Pharaoh's heart had hardened to the point where, after nine other plagues, God decided to act decisively to deliver his people. Instructions were given to the Jewish people to kill an unblemished lamb, cook it, and eat it at twilight. They were to eat the meal fully dressed and ready to travel. The blood from the sacrificed lamb was put on the doorposts and the lintels so the death angel would see the blood on the doorposts of the Jewish families and pass by.

Certainly the first Passover was not celebrated with festivity but with great solemnity. In future years, once the Israelites were settled in their homeland, the meal became a time to remember God's great provision and to celebrate it joyously. In fact, God said, "This day shall be a memorial to you, and you shall celebrate it . . . as a permanent ordinance" (Exod. 12:14). The Passover became the most important Hebrew holy day.

Most people in our society no longer connect the concept of holiday with holy day. In previous generations Americans made this connection and, even amid the secularized version of the holy day, had sought to retain some of the religious element. Perhaps the only totally unifying holiday in America today, filled with the kind of festivity that characterized the Passover, is Super Bowl Sunday. A two-week buildup, elaborately covered by the media, climaxes on a January Sunday afternoon and evening when friends and family gather to give their attention to a televised football game and food. This is not a criticism of football but an observation that most people never approach the fervor of a religious festival apart from Super Bowl Sunday.

Historically, the Passover has been celebrated by Jewish people in an interesting way. At least ten people were required for a celebration of the meal. The head of the house, once everyone was in place, pronounced a blessing on the festival and the wine, and invited everyone to drink the first cup. He quoted from Exodus 6:6–7, "I will bring you out from under the burdens of the Egyptians." Food was then brought in. It consisted of unleavened bread, bitter herbs, greens, stewed fruit, and roast lamb. The youngest son would then ask the father why this day was so special. The father would recount the redemption from Egypt. Then the first part of the Hallel, Psalms 113–15, was sung. The second cup of wine was poured and more of Exodus 6 was quoted, "I will rid you out of their bondage" (v. 6 KJV). A blessing on the bread followed, after which the bread was broken and given to all to eat, along with the bitter herbs and stewed fruit. Next, the lamb was served.

A third cup was offered with a prayer of thanksgiving and more of Exodus 6:6, "I will redeem you with an outstretched arm" (KJV), and the people sang the second part of the Hallel, Psalms 116–18. Finally, a fourth cup of wine was poured with the words, "I will take you as my own people, and I will be your God" (6:7 NIV).

Far from being hurried, this meal was eaten leisurely with great joy and much humor. Some years ago, while I was a graduate student at New York University, my wife and I were invited by a fellow student to participate in his family's Passover celebration. My friend, Avi, was an orthodox rabbi. One aspect of the Passover not commonly known is that Jewish families are to try to have Gentile guests at the meal. As we enjoyed the leisurely meal, we were aware of Avi's wife who diligently served all of the courses, hurrying to make sure everyone was served just so. Near the end of the meal, the Jews always say, "Next year in Jerusalem." As Avi and his family approached this part of the meal, little did they know that the humor for the evening

> *Only knowing about Jesus is like having bread*
> *in one's hand while continuing to starve to death.*

had not ended. While everyone else uttered, "Next year in Jerusalem," one exhausted female voice was heard, "Next year in Acapulco!"

The Passion Meal

Even though their meal was not in Acapulco, Jesus' disciples looked forward to Passover with Jesus. Mark 14:12 indicates that they approached Jesus, asking where he wanted them to go to prepare the meal. No doubt they relished the thought of the meal not only because it was a rich feast but also because it would provide opportunity to hear the Master speak about the exodus. Little did they know what was to happen.

In response to their request, Jesus gave specific instructions. Two of them were to go into the city, find a man carrying a pitcher of water, follow him and say to the owners of the house, "The Teacher says, 'Where is My guest room in which I may eat the Passover with My disciples?'" (Mark 14:14).

Some have speculated about these events. Was it totally coincidental that the disciples would find such a man who would willingly lend his home, or had Jesus prearranged the event? Some have suggested that the meal was served in the upper room in the home of Mary, John Mark's mother, and perhaps Mark himself was the man carrying the pitcher. Certainly the man would be noticed because in Jewish society men generally did not carry pitchers of water. However the arrangements were made, Jesus, during his most stressful week on earth, seemed to have time to attend to details.

His instructions led the two disciples to an appropriate place. If, indeed, the Last Supper took place in the upper room that would later be the site of the pentecostal event described in Acts 2, it was probably a large room accessed from the outside. It was furnished and ready for the meal.

We should pause to consider the courage of the owner in allowing Jesus to use the room. Jesus was a fugitive. It was no secret that he was a wanted man, and the home owner had nothing to gain by hosting Jesus. Many Christians, perhaps most of us, would think twice if we were in the same situation. I recall a Sunday evening testimony service when a Christian executive stood and quoted Psalm 103:2, "Bless the LORD, O my soul, and forget none of His benefits." Then he concluded his testimony by saying, "I like those benefits." One hopes he was referring to the spiritual benefits of knowing the Lord, but who knows?

In all likelihood the host for this important meal was himself a follower of Jesus because the disciples, when requesting the room, were to refer to Jesus as, "the Teacher." At any rate, he offered his best room and made sure it had ample provisions. The booklet, *My Heart Christ's Home,*[1] compares Christian lives to a house with a number of rooms from which different activities and functions are performed. Each of us is encouraged to analyze his or her life, asking where Christ is welcomed and which rooms are under lock and key. Is Christ truly at home in us? That is, does he have full reign within the house? Or have we cordoned off areas of our lives from his presence for selfish purposes?

Two thousand years after the Last Supper we look on it as a momentous event of Christian history. For the owner of the upper room its significance was unknown. Nevertheless, his faithfulness in making provisions for Christ resulted in one of the most holy moments ever to be experienced throughout history and throughout the world.

Mark writes that the disciples prepared the Passover. To do this they procured a spotless lamb. The Passover meal at that time was personally involving, and the people who brought lambs to the temple were required to slay their own lamb and make sure they caught the blood in a bowl held by the priest. They would then take the blood and splash it on the altar, which symbolized the doorpost. The carcass of the animal was then flayed and given back to the worshipper. The lamb was roasted on an open fire and served with unleavened bread to symbolize the haste in which it was prepared during the first Passover experience. (Leavened bread had to rise and took more time, whereas unleavened bread could be made quickly.) A bowl of salt water, symbolizing the Red Sea, as well as bit-

> *Many Christians, perhaps most of us, would have to think twice before taking Jesus without his benefits.*

ter herbs symbolizing the adverse circumstances of the Jews during the first Passover, rounded out the meal.

Having returned to the upper room, the disciples then joined the others, reclining around a low, U-shaped table. They proceeded through the Passover ceremony, and ate the lamb toward the latter part of the supper.

Chew on This!

During that time Jesus became troubled in his spirit, according to John's Gospel, and said, "One of you will betray Me" (13:21), without indicating who it was. The moment must have been more dramatic, however, when Jesus said it was the one to whom he would give bread (v. 26). To eat with someone was to be in open fellowship and, therefore, to be a trusted companion. The shock of this pronouncement resulted not in accusations, but appropriate introspection as the disciples each looked within, wondering whether it could be he. Up to this point in their communal life there seemed to be complete trust. What if this happened in one of our small group Bible studies today? What if someone announced that one of us would turn against Jesus? Would we be quick to accuse and point a finger at others, or would each of us appropriately examine our own hearts?

The betrayal Jesus described was not simply a matter of abandonment. The term *betray* means *deliver up* by turning Jesus over to the authorities as a criminal. Even so, we find Jesus beseeching Judas first to understand the gravity of his act, and second, to do it quickly. John's Gospel indicates that Jesus allowed some of the disciples closest to him to know that Judas would be the betrayer by handing him the next morsel. After Jesus gave the morsel to Judas, Satan entered Judas and he left. Most of the disciples thought Judas was leaving to attend to a charitable ministry.

Jesus' comments also give insight into his total submission to God's plan for his life. He said, "The Son of Man is to go, just as it is written of Him" (Mark 14:21). It is likely that Jesus was thinking here of Isaiah 53:7:

> He was oppressed and He was afflicted,
> Yet He did not open His mouth;
> Like a lamb that is led to slaughter,
> And like a sheep that is silent before its shearers,
> So He did not open His mouth.

What a remarkable parallel. Earlier, two of the disciples left the group to slaughter a lamb, splash its blood on the altar, and bring it to the feast to remember God's deliverance of the Jews during the exodus. Now Judas has left the group to sacrifice the Lamb of God.

The disciples finished the meal, "and after singing a hymn, they went out to the Mount of Olives" (Mark 14:26). At the time, they were not prepared to grapple with the implications of all they had seen and heard. But we have no excuse for not carefully considering these events and understanding as best we can the substitutionary atonement of Jesus Christ. Often evangelists encourage people simply to receive Jesus—as if it were no more than receiving a nice gift. But this leaves a very shallow understanding of what actually took place at Calvary and why it took place.

Two Meals, One Meaning

The parallels between the Passover and the passion meal deepen our understanding of the atonement. The Israelites were the participants in the Passover. They were helpless, sinful, enslaved, and death-bound. All sinners are beneficiaries of the passion meal, and have the opportunity to be saved, even though they, likewise, are helpless, sinful, enslaved, and death-bound. In both meals God, holy, just, and loving, is behind the scenes and directs the events. In the Passover meal an innocent lamb was slaughtered as a substitute to bear the guilt of the sinners. In the passion meal, Jesus Christ with his "precious blood, as of a lamb unblemished and spotless" (1 Peter 1:19) is the sacrifice. The blood of the Passover lamb guaranteed rightness before God when the act was exercised in faith.

The blood of Christ is able to cleanse the whole person from dead works to serve the living God (see Heb. 9:14–15). The exodus after the Passover enabled the Jewish people to escape their bondage and enter a new life. The passion of Jesus enables Christians to escape the bondage of sin and enter newness of life to serve Christ now and be with him forever.

The Last Supper began as a celebration of the Passover, observed in the traditional way. Jesus gave it a very untraditional interpretation by making a connection between the Passover and his impending passion. As we think more deeply about it, why did Jesus not compare himself to the sacrificed lamb? Instead, he took bread and said, "This is my body." Wouldn't you think that the symbolism of being the sacrifice would have been better made by comparing himself to the lamb? He was known to be the Lamb of God. Perhaps his reason for not drawing the comparison was that the lamb had a strictly Jewish significance. Bread, however, is common. It is the staff of life and food for every person. Jesus' sacrifice was not simply to be for one ethnic group in a small region of the world. All nations, all races, all people groups, all areas of the world were to benefit from his death.

Bread That Lasts

In John 6, as an earlier Passover season was approaching, Jesus was in a remote place with his disciples ministering to many people. Philip panicked about provisions for the meal, but Andrew brought to Jesus a lad who had five barley loaves and two fish. After seating the people, Jesus took the loaves from the boy, gave thanks and distributed to those who were seated. He distributed the fish in a similar manner. Everyone ate to their heart's content and the disciples gathered twelve baskets of fragments that were left over. Over five thousand men and their families were fed from what John calls "this sign." This event apparently confused the people because later they were trying to compare this experience with that of their fathers in the wilderness in the days of Moses. They quoted from Psalm 78:24, "He gave them bread out of heaven to eat" (John 6:31). Jesus told them not to seek the bread of Moses but the "true bread out of heaven" (v. 32) that the Father was giving and that would give life to the world, not simply to one group of people. Then Jesus made a bold declaration, "I

> **Earlier, two of the disciples left the group
> to slaughter a lamb. Now Judas has left the group
> to sacrifice the Lamb of God.**

am the bread of life; he who comes to Me shall not hunger, and he who believes in Me shall never thirst" (John 6:35).

Others proclaimed Jesus to be the Lamb of God. He proclaimed himself to be the bread that came down out of heaven. He went on to say, "If anyone eats of this bread, he shall live forever; and the bread also which I shall give for the life of the world is My flesh" (John 6:51). The metaphor was then expanded to include his blood.

> He who eats My flesh and drinks My blood has eternal life, and I will raise him up on the last day. For My flesh is true food, and My blood is true drink. He who eats My flesh and drinks My blood abides in Me, and I in him.
>
> John 6:54–56

The symbolism of his body and blood being consumed in the passion meal was not a new thought to Jesus during that last evening. Several years earlier, as indicated in John 6, Jesus anticipated being the body and blood for the world. As God's Holy Spirit revealed these words, imagine what was going on in John's mind as he wrote about the feeding of the five thousand after having heard Jesus' words at the passion meal.

One of the most important truths from this event is the statement in John 6:35 that whoever partakes of Jesus has his spiritual appetite satisfied. God has given every person a spiritual appetite. Theologians have called this the *imago dei*, the image of God, including the God-shaped void in every person. No other substance can fulfill that appetite. The spiritual hunger continues until God fills the void in a person's life. Some people, however, repress that hunger and deny it because they will not believe. Jesus knew this bread must be eaten to be of any use. Only knowing about Jesus is like having bread in one's hand while continuing to starve to death. Eating the bread expresses faith in its nutrient value; partaking of Christ by trusting him for salvation expresses faith in the saving merit of his death. Those who do partake have eternal life. Those who hunger and thirst for righteousness will be satisfied.

Covenant Blood

If Jesus compared his body to bread because bread is a universal substance, why did he choose the fruit of the vine to symbolize his blood? Why didn't he choose water, a universal substance? The reason is that wine symbolizes life. Life is in the blood making it the most valuable element in the universe. We are told that without the shedding of blood there is no forgiveness of sin (Heb. 9:22). Cain was guilty before God because he tried to appease God with a bloodless sacrifice. Abel's sacrifices were acceptable because they included the shedding of blood. Wine symbolizes blood because it is a dynamic liquid; it ferments. Water, left to sit, will stagnate.

As Jesus offered his friends the cup of wine he said, "This is My blood of the covenant" (Mark 14:24). The word covenant is rich in Jewish literature. It connotes an agreement or a bargain. The old covenant was a two-way agreement.

> Now then, if you will indeed obey My voice and keep My covenant, then you shall be My own possession among all the peoples, for all the earth is Mine; and you shall be to Me a kingdom of priests and a holy nation.
>
> Exodus 19:5–6

This covenant required obedience to the law.

The new covenant that Jesus gave is a one-way agreement, like a will. In fact, the word *new* indicates not that the covenant being offered by Jesus was new in time *(neos)* but new in quality *(kainos)*. The new covenant is not a revision or an updating of the old covenant. It is not a restatement. It is an entirely different kind of covenant—a one-way agreement foretold in Jeremiah 31:31–34:

> "Behold, days are coming," declares the LORD, "when I will make a new covenant with the house of Israel and the house of Judah. . . . this is the covenant which I will make with the house of Israel after those days," declares the LORD, "I will put My law within them, and on their heart I will write it; and I will be their God, and they shall be

My people. . . . for I will forgive their iniquity, and their sin I will remember no more."

Notice that this Old Testament promise of the new covenant contains no conditions. God would do it and he would do it without our help.

This is what makes Christianity unique. It is based on the pure and total sacrifice of Jesus Christ for us. His sacrifice meets God's requirements for justice because he made atonement for our sin. God's mercy is also expressed because he himself bore our punishment. And while we may do nothing to supplement the sacrifice of

> *Those who demonstrate a deep, godly sorrow over their sins will advance faithfully, far more than others whose repentance is shallow.*

Christ, which Scripture calls the gift of God, we are expected to believe in the efficacy of that gift and humbly receive it.

Actions and Attitudes

Christ bid the disciples at the Last Supper to "Take, eat; this is My body" (Matt. 26:26), and to "Drink from it, all of you" (v. 27). He provided the meal; they were exhorted to partake of it. Partaking of Christ involves both action and attitudes. Our first action is to admit and repent of our sin. The underlying attitude must be sorrow. After hearing scores, if not hundreds, of testimonies by Christians who walked faithfully with Christ throughout the years and by others who wandered away for a time, I am convinced that the depth of repentance at the time of conversion may determine a person's faithfulness in walking with Christ as well as the rate of growth they experience in him. Those who demonstrate a deep, godly sorrow over their sins will advance faithfully, far more than others whose repentance is shallow.

Second, we must acknowledge or confess Christ as Savior and Lord as we are exhorted in Romans 10:9–10, undergirding that with faith. Furthermore, we are to trust him for salvation and to stop trying to please God through our own efforts. The underlying attitude is humility, recognizing that we have nothing to offer him. As the classic hymn "Rock of Ages" says, "Nothing in my hand I bring, simply to thy cross I cling."

Our last act is to actually ask him to be our Savior and Lord, undergirding that with sincerity. These three acts are not meant to suggest certain steps—they are all one transaction—but the actions and attitudes must go together as we partake of Christ. Leviticus 16 gives interesting instructions to the Jewish priests for conducting the ceremony of atonement. Aaron (the chief priest) was to take two goats and present them before the Lord and cast lots for the two goats. One lot was cast for the Lord and one for a scapegoat. The goat that received the lot cast for the Lord was declared to be a sin offering and was sacrificed accordingly. The scapegoat, on the other hand, was taken by the priest who would

> lay both hands on the head of the live goat and confess over it all the wickedness and rebellion of the Israelites—all their sins—and put them on the goat's head. He shall send the goat away into the desert in the care of a man appointed for the task. The goat will carry on itself all their sins. . . .
>
> Leviticus 16:21–22 NIV

The analogy regarding Christ's sacrifice may not be perfect, but the ritual clearly involved the shedding of blood and the transfer of sin to be borne by another. More important to Moses, however, was the reason for this annual ceremony. "It is to be a sabbath of solemn rest for you, *that you may humble your souls*" (Lev. 16:31, emphasis added).

I believe that ultimately people choose to reject Jesus Christ for only one reason. They are unwilling to humble their souls. People talk about the impossibility of believing in the miraculous elements of the Christian gospel. What a smoke screen! Anyone who thinks is aware that the universe, despite our advanced scientific knowledge, is filled with mystery. The reason people choose to reject the benefits of Christ is usually the desire not to admit their utter helplessness, their dire need, and their total dependency on someone else. During Lent the various spiritual disciplines are for the sole purpose of helping us humble our souls.

Only the humble hunger and thirst for righteousness. Many people hunger and thirst for other things: wealth, power, fame, prestige, comfort, and so forth, which the bread and the wine, the body and the blood, do not give. The bread and the wine, the body and the blood do give righteousness, and only righteousness satisfies.

Group Study

Read Mark 14:21–31 and John 13:1–30.

1. What factors may have contributed to the "coincidental" timing of Passover and the Last Supper?
2. The Synoptic Gospels do not give the account of the foot washing. What was the main lesson of this episode recorded by John? What character qualities did Jesus exemplify?
3. Why did Jesus so eagerly anticipate the Last Supper (see Luke 22:15)? How is this intensity similar to the beatitude of hungering and thirsting for righteousness?
4. Why did Jesus precede the meal by announcing that one of the twelve would betray him? How did this prediction affect the mood of the meal?
5. Without having a previous understanding of the communion, how might the disciples first have interpreted the statements about "my body" and "my blood"?
6. How does John's account of Jesus indicating the betrayer (13:21–27) dramatize the event?
7. How does the Passover meal typify the Last Supper?
8. How are the communion services that you participate in re-enactments of the original Lord's Supper?
9. Why in your opinion did Jesus institute the Lord's Supper as a feast to be celebrated until he comes again? How does this celebration affect Christian community?
10. How do the verbs "broke it," referring to the bread, and "poured out," referring to the wine, describe what would happen to Jesus and what should happen to us?
11. How does the Last Supper prefigure the messianic banquet (see Luke 22:28–30)?
12. How does the communion service keep calling us to remember our sin as well as remember the Lord?

The Garden Prayer

Mark 14:32–41

"My soul is overwhelmed with sorrow to the point of death," he said to them. "Stay here and keep watch."

Mark 14:34 NIV

Blessed are those who mourn.

For many people a garden is a place of joy. Avid gardeners eagerly turn the crusty, neglected ground to find fresh, fertile soil ready to nurture the seeds of fruits, vegetables, plants, and flowers. The gardener delights in cultivating these plants.

For others, a garden is a place of tranquility and serenity. It is a place of beautifully manicured grounds, neatly trimmed hedges, symmetrically planted trees, gentle flowing streams, strategically placed benches, and small animals and birds. A garden fosters a spiritually and emotionally rich setting.

As I was growing up, the garden meant one thing—pulling weeds on Saturdays. Thus, gardens present a variety of pictures to different people.

41

In the Bible, the two most famous gardens are associated with sin. The Garden of Eden, where the first humans were formed and learned to walk with God, was the setting for the spiritual downfall of humanity. Adam and Eve sinned against their Maker and were expelled from the garden.

The Garden of Gethsemane, which on earlier occasions had proven to be a place of spiritual retreat for Jesus and his followers, became a place of intense suffering as Jesus vainly prayed to escape the hour of judgment.

Leaving the ecstasy of the upper room, where the Passover and the passion meal had been enjoyed, Jesus and the disciples journeyed across the Kidron Valley to the Garden of Gethsemane on the Mount of Olives, soon to be the site of official action against Jesus.

Blessed Are Those Who Mourn

The night spent in the garden would be the dark night of Jesus' soul. Emotionally strong, Jesus would experience soul-shaking terror. Lest we think of the garden prayer as a pity party, we need to see that this was not a totally unique experience for Jesus. On other occasions he had mourned the damning effects of sin, such as when he lamented Jerusalem's plight (Matt. 23:37–39) and when he wept over the death of Lazarus (John 11:35).

Mourning can be self-serving, but the biblical concept does not include self-pity. To mourn is to be grieved about a sorrowful condition or the sorry state of the world in general. For the follower of Jesus, mourning begins as the sorrow of repentance over the loss of one's innocence, righteousness, and self-respect. But mourning is also the Christlike response to all arenas of life where sin holds power and results in judgment and death.

Old Testament saints were often seen to mourn, expressing it in various ways—sackcloth, ashes, shaved heads, torn clothes. Honest sorrow, for the right reasons, is a godly virtue. We mourn best when we experience the reality of life as God sees it. Much in the world today should cause the spiritually sensitive Christian to mourn. Jesus' garden experience exemplified perfect mourning. Look closely at this passage and see not only a sorrowing soul but also a sensitive and submissive soul.

En route to the Mount of Olives Jesus told the disciples that they would all fall away from him as predicted in Zechariah 13:7. Peter, never one to avoid asserting his own self-confidence, vowed that even though all others might fall away, he would not. We would think that Peter's bravado would have been squelched by Jesus' reply that Peter would, that very night before a rooster crowed twice, deny Jesus three times. Nevertheless, Peter insisted that he would not deny Jesus even if it meant dying with him. The other disciples took up the chorus and pledged their devotion.

The passage we are considering contains one of the better known sayings of Scripture, "The spirit is willing, but the flesh is weak" (Mark 14:38). We recite this proverb in day-to-day living, usually humorously to excuse minor spiritual misdemeanors, such as not staying on a diet, watching too much television, or not accomplishing a household project. Originally, Jesus uttered the statement to the disciples, who were unable to stay awake and pray during an hour of testing. But the phrase also expressed a reality Jesus was experiencing in his inner life in the Garden of Gethsemane. His desire was to avoid the horror of the cross. His flesh recoiled at the grisly criminal death that awaited him. In his spirit, however, Jesus said, "Not my will but yours be done."

Prayer Pointers

Why did Jesus go to the garden on this fateful night? Simply to pray. Prayer is the retreat of all people in times of crisis. Emergencies make pray-ers out of agnostics. But for Jesus prayer was not merely an emergency exercise. Look with me at six things that give color to the account in the garden.

The Place

The place where Jesus prayed was one that he had frequented on other occasions for the same purpose. He was no stranger to Gethsemane, a garden probably owned by friends in Jerusalem, perhaps by the family of John Mark. The word *Gethsemane* means *oil press,* indicating that the garden was an olive grove. Those who have toured the Holy Land including the Mount of Olives have doubtlessly seen gnarly old trees that may have been witness to the prayer of our Lord and his subsequent arrest. For Jesus, however, the garden was chiefly a place of prayer. It was his "closet," which he entered to spend precious personal time with his Father.

Bill McCartney, head football coach of the University of Colorado Buffaloes, came as an adult to know Christ. His spiritual growth has been a delight to follow. Because of the outstanding success of his football teams, he has achieved national prominence. Not one to hide his light under a bushel, Coach McCartney has been outspoken on social and spiritual issues and has created an organization to encourage men to be "Promise Keepers" in their relationships to God, family, and church. Several years ago, the McCartney's designed a new home to be constructed in the Boulder, Colorado, area. In exhorting a group of pastors about the importance of prayer in their ministries, the coach mentioned that he had designed one room to be his prayer closet. Each day he enters this room and spends considerable time before God. McCartney confides that God has told him that for every hour spent on his knees in prayer, God will give him one man, meaning the salvation of one man.

Maybe your prayer closet is simply an easy chair or perhaps a place where you kneel, a special room, a special place outdoors. The type of place and its location are unimportant. Having a place for regular prayer is important. Praying there is more important.

The People

The people with Jesus were divided into two groups. Eight of his followers were left near the gate of the garden with no particular instructions. Three, Peter, James, and John, accompanied Jesus deeper into the garden. Why these three? For one thing, they were the ones who had seen the glorified Jesus in the transfiguration. Now they would behold his agony. They were certainly his most intimate friends.

Furthermore, these three had openly assumed responsibility to share in the destiny of Jesus. We have already referred to Peter's strong vow (Mark 14:29, 31). Earlier (Mark 10:38–40), brothers James and John, wanting to sit on the right and left sides of Jesus in his glory, vowed that they would be able to drink the cup that Jesus drank and be baptized with the baptism with which he would be baptized. Jesus affirmed that they would indeed experience those things, and now he was giving them a first sip from his cup. He instructed them to remain with him and keep watch. They were

> *For the follower of Jesus, mourning begins as the sorrow of repentance over the loss of one's innocence, righteousness, and self-respect.*

called to vigilance because Jesus knew the chance of their failing in the hour of testing was very great.

We may want to criticize these sleepy disciples, but first we should ask where we would have been on that night. The prayer habits of most Christians suggest we would have been with the eight who were not in the prayer meeting. About the three, Jesus could say "the spirit is willing." Could he say that about you in terms of your prayer life?

The Purpose

The purpose of their going to the garden was to pray. Why did Jesus need to pray at this time? He indicated that his soul was deeply grieved, even to the point of death (Mark 14:34). Emotionally, he was distressed and grieving. One writer suggests that these words indicate the utmost degree of unbounded horror and suffering, a terrified surprise and shuddering awe. The words, *unto death* indicate that his soul was so troubled that death was next.[1] Certainly Jesus was in touch with reality. This was no false paranoia he was experiencing.

We might ask, If Jesus, the Son of God, needed to pray, how much more do we? A prerequisite for such deep prayer is being awake to the spiritual realities around us. Recently my friend, who held a very responsible job, was dismissed from his position primarily because he became out of touch with the realities around him. While no one doubted his ability or his motivation, many of his board members were amazed at the external confusion, controversy, and mistrust that surrounded his leadership and from which he seemed to be emotionally detached. Naivete is not a commendable quality, especially for Christians. Jesus exhorted his followers to "keep watch" on many other occasions (see, for example, Mark 13:33–37). Christians who want to be meaningfully involved in history and the world on God's behalf will develop a deep prayer life as they learn to stay awake to the spiritual realities around them.

The Posture

Notice also the posture of Jesus in this time of prayer. He fell to the ground. As he knelt and prayed his sweat was like drops of blood (Luke 22:44). Mark's account that Jesus fell to the ground suggests that Jesus did not just lie prone, but perhaps sort of staggered—getting up, falling to the ground, getting up, falling again—indicating great anguish and misery. Certainly during this time Jesus was as earnest and intense as anyone could be.

One of my heros of the faith from the twentieth century is A. W. Tozer, widely known for his books on devotion and piety. *The Knowledge of the Holy* and *The Pursuit of God* have been especially formative in my life. Those who knew Tozer, who died in 1963, were aware that his powerful, prophetic preaching flowed from a deep personal experience with God. Those who visited his study saw an oriental rug that was nearly threadbare in the middle from hours of Tozer's lying prostrate before God in worship and prayer. Not many will achieve that degree of intensity, but thank God for examples like this that keep us properly humble and motivate us in that direction.

The Petition

The petition of Jesus was a conditional prayer. He asked that, "if it were possible" (Mark 14:36), the Father would release him from the cup he was destined to drink. His prayer acknowledged the overarching priority of God's will. Mark 14:35 mentions that he prayed that "the hour" might pass him by. That hour would become the fulcrum of history, a foretaste of the day of the Lord when God will thoroughly judge sin. Jesus could foresee that sin being meted out on him. The cup he referred to in verse 36 was clearly God's wrath against sin. This is the cup from which James and John naively agreed to drink, which they obviously could not do since they were comfortably asleep. How easily God's people make promises, even vows, only to find that "the spirit is willing but the flesh is weak." As Ecclesiastes 5:5 says, "It is better that you should not vow than that you should vow and not pay."

The Plan

The backdrop to all this activity in the garden was the plan, God's plan of redemption. The Father's answer to Jesus' request had to be negative. His divine, eternal plan called for the fulfillment of this crucial event. Jesus was the only chance humanity had for salvation. An apocryphal story tells of the angels' questioning God the Father shortly after the incarnation of Jesus. Why had God chosen this particular method to save humanity? After giving an appropriate response to the angels, God was then asked by them, "And if it fails, what is your backup plan?" The response of the Father was, "I have no backup. This is my only plan."

Being fully God and knowing the necessity of the atonement, why did Jesus pray to be exempt from this cup? Because he was also fully man. It is important for us to know that while his human will sought one thing, he had already determined to obey God. We may certainly petition God for our desire, but wanting to know and obey God's plan should undergird all our prayers.

Human Help Wanted

While desiring to pray was surely the primary motive for Jesus' going to the garden, evidently he also wanted human support while he was there. He need not have taken Peter, James, and John with him to his special place of prayer, but he did. No doubt he knew it was going to be an intense time. The garden experience highlights the human side of Jesus. Everyone in times of great stress and sorrow benefits from the presence of a few close friends who are understanding.

Jesus was modeling an important element for the church that he came to establish. God's people have always been a community. Sharing in times of joy and sorrow is part of the character of that community. The lyric from a once popular song, "I get by with a little help from my friends," is not an entirely secular notion. Jesus intended us to be interdependent in a positive way. Charles Colson, in his book *The Body,* notes the following ideas about the church.

> Surveys show that the number one thing people look for in a church is fellowship. But what most modern westerners seek is a far cry from what the Bible describes and what the early church practiced. No term in the Christian lexicon is more abused than fellowship.
>
> To some it means . . . the warm, affirming, "hot tub" religion that soothes our frayed nerves and provides relief from the battering of everyday life. For many others, fellowship means no more than coming together for church events. Instead of happy hours at the club, they have theirs in the fellowship hall (a name which, by the way, contributes to the wrong impression).[2]

The fellowship Jesus needed at this time was far deeper than most of us are prepared to offer. Did he expect them to share in his suffering by sharing in his cup? Did he expect them to share in the cross-bearing that he referred to in Mark 8:34? If so, he was disappointed. Paul later affirmed that one of the greatest privileges a Christian might experience is to share in the fellowship of the sufferings of Jesus (Phil. 3:10). The disciples at this moment, however, enjoyed fellowship with one another in sleep. Three times Jesus

> *Christians who want to be meaningfully involved in history and the world on God's behalf will develop a deep prayer life as they learn to stay awake to the spiritual realities around them.*

admonished them for sleeping while they were to be on watch. How strange that these men, who so recently had proclaimed they would die for Jesus, could not stay awake one hour for him. It must have stung Peter to hear Jesus address him as Simon in this situation because surely he did not deserve the name Peter, meaning rock.

Before we condemn Peter and the others too much, we need to examine our own lives. Our sensitivity level may also be quite low and our prayer stamina may be no greater than theirs. We are as susceptible as they to the willingness of the spirit and the weakness of flesh. Christians are complex creatures. Even the great apostle Paul admitted that in his flesh nothing good existed, for when his spirit wanted to do something good, his flesh, having within it an evil principle, would war against his spirit and make him a prisoner to sin (Rom. 7:8–25). In fact, "the flesh sets its desire against the Spirit, and the Spirit against the flesh; for these are in opposition to one another, so that you may not do the things that you please" (Gal. 5:17). This complexity can be overruled only by the indwelling Holy Spirit.

Many well-intentioned Christians have tried the route of self-discipline. Elaborate discipleship programs have been created to assist Christians in spiritual disciplines that will help them gain mastery over the flesh. My experience and the testimony of others is that such an approach is futile. The human will is not strong enough to defeat the appetites of the flesh. Paul warned the Galatian believers that they should not seek spiritual victory by resorting to confidence in the flesh. He reminded them, "Are you so foolish? Having begun by the Spirit, are you now being perfected by the flesh?" (Gal. 3:3).

We must pause to notice that living by the Spirit does not always mean being comfortable. During the hours of agony in the garden, Jesus undoubtedly was filled with the Spirit. Nevertheless, he went through the shadow of the valley of death. The disciples were fast asleep, presumably quite comfortable. Later they would pay the price for not having prayed. They were not prepared for the testing that came their way—exactly as Jesus had anticipated when he admonished them to keep watching and praying so that they would not come into temptation. Even in his moment of greatest need, he continued to teach them and call them into spiritual maturity—not for his sake but for theirs.

Cursed on the Cross

We see also in this text that Jesus desired to avoid the cross. Far from having a martyr's complex and wanting to die as a hero, Jesus, at age thirty-three, did not want to die. He knew, however, that his primary mission for coming to the earth could not be fulfilled unless he died a sacrificial death. Nevertheless, he did not want to die. In the prime of life, Jesus knew there was so much more that he could do.

For him the cross entailed four negative elements. First, it meant suffering. Crucifixion on a Roman cross was one of the most torturous means of death. I'll not describe it here. Perhaps you have heard or read accounts of the slow, painful, agonizing death that characterized crucifixion. Dreading the pain from the crucifixion experience was, by itself, enough to give Jesus the deep anguish of soul he experienced in the garden.

> ***Jesus went to the garden to be with the Father.***
> ***But he sensed the shadow of hell***
> ***rather than the gates of heaven.***

Second, dying on a cross meant great shame. Old Testament Scripture taught "If a man has committed a sin worthy of death, and he is put to death, and you hang him on a tree . . . he who is hanged is accursed of God" (Deut. 21:22–23). Jews throughout Judea, Samaria, Galilee, and wherever this story was told would consider Jesus a rightfully condemned criminal if he died in shame on a cross. He would be judged a fraud, and his messianic supporters would have been convinced that he was a false Messiah.

As severe as the suffering and shame of the cross were for Jesus, separation from God entailed even greater suffering and shame. None of us can begin to appreciate the unity that exists between the members of the Godhead. Throughout eternity the Three-in-One has existed in the closest possible communion. But for six agonizing hours, as Jesus hung on the cross, the Trinity was dissolved while the Father turned his back on the sin-cursed Son. In the garden, Jesus could still address God as "Abba, Father" indicating the intimacy that existed between them (Mark 14:36 NIV). But on the cross Jesus called out, "My God, my God, why have you forsaken me?" (Mark 15:33 NIV).

The dreadful sorrow and anxiety that motivated him to pray for the cup to be removed was not motivated merely by fear but also

You are devaluing the cross, stripping the crucifixion of its meaning, rendering God a blood-guilty criminal and Jesus a pathetic victim.

by the horror of alienation from the Father. Ironically, the garden experience was supposed to be an interlude for Jesus to be with the Father before the betrayal. But during Jesus' prayer, he sensed for the first time the shadow of hell before him rather than the gates of heaven opening to him, and he staggered.

Most stressful for him as he prayed in the garden, however, was the sense of the world's sin being placed on him. Perfect holiness was about to be smothered—the innocent one being condemned with the sin and guilt of all humanity.

That humans needed his sacrifice Jesus had no doubt. At that very moment men were on the path up the Mount of Olives to destroy him. Their names were jealousy, pride, unbelief, hatred, greed, and so forth. Nevertheless, the prospect of bearing sin terrified him. No wonder he asked if there would be any other way for God's will to be accomplished. Francis Schaeffer describes it this way:

> Father, can't there be another way? Father, can't you think of another way of salvation for the people? Father, is this really the only way to save people from the results of their sin?
>
> It was a breathless moment in the universe. The angels had been waiting for the victory to be won over Satan. The people who had died through the centuries were waiting in Hades for the price actually to be paid and the door to be opened for them to go out to Paradise. Satan and the demons had tried to hinder Jesus from living, tried to kill him as a baby, tried to tempt him to sin. This moment of decision, the importance of the answer, meant total defeat to Satan.

Only One Way

Interestingly, so many people today shrink from the idea of there being only one way of salvation, but think of it—if there were any other way, the Father would have been needlessly cruel, even immoral, in putting his Son through this experience. To those misguided souls who in their good intentions want to affirm other ways of being right with God than through Jesus Christ, we say, "You are devaluing the cross, stripping the crucifixion of its meaning, rendering God a blood-guilty criminal and Jesus a pathetic victim." There is only one way to atone for sin, only one spotless Lamb of God, only one provision for salvation. Had there been any other way, don't you believe the Father would have quickly harkened to the plea of his perfect Son and rescued him from the hands of cruel men?

More than anything else—more than desiring to pray, more than desiring human support, more than desiring to avoid the cross— Jesus desired to do God's will. Overriding any concern for his own well-being, Jesus pursued the will of God, even to exhausting his last drop of blood. Why? He knew there was no other way to achieve atonement. God's eternal plan for all creation, especially mankind, was dependent on his faithfully fulfilling the will of God. He was willing to suffer so we wouldn't have to suffer. He was willing to take our filthy sin so we could be cleansed. He was willing to be separated from God so we would never have to be. He was willing to go naked to the cross so that we could be clothed in the white linen of his righteousness. He was willing to die so we could have life.

Just as centuries earlier rebellion in a garden had brought death's reign over mankind, so now submission in a garden was the beginning of the death of death. One of the great Puritan writers, John Owen, wrote about this in his book, *The Death of Death in the Death of Christ*. The Book of Revelation calls death the final enemy of mankind. That enemy was defeated by Jesus' death because the result was Jesus' resurrection. All who become spiritually alive in him will experience that same great victory. No wonder Jesus promised that those who mourn will be comforted!

One of the great Old Testament names of God is Jehovah-jireh— the Lord will provide. This name was given to a special place where an altar was built to God and a sacrifice was about to be made (see Gen. 22:1–18). Isaac—the miraculous son promised to the aged Abraham and Sarah, the one from whom all the nations of the earth were to be blessed—innocently carried the fuel on which he would be sacrificed, wondering to his father where they would get the lamb for a burnt offering. After building the altar, arranging the wood, binding his son, and laying him on the altar on top of the wood, Abraham raised the knife to slay Isaac. However, Abraham heard his name and the command not to harm Isaac called from heaven. God was pleased with Abraham's obedience and his willingness to put to death his most treasured possession. God was pleased that Abraham did not argue, did not remind God of his promise, and did not discuss a compromise.

Even before unbinding Isaac, Abraham captured God's provision, a ram caught in the bushes by its horns. Abraham took the ram and offered it as a burnt offering in the place of his son, and then named the place Jehovah-jireh.

The symbolism of the story is powerful. God provided a sacrifice so that the son need not perish. How apt it would be to consider the Garden of Gethsemane God's new Jehovah-jireh, for it was there that Jesus was caught in the thicket and became the Father's provision to atone for the sins of the world. There he ruefully mourned the death and damnation brought by sin. He mourned; we are comforted.

Group Study

Read Mark 14:32–41 and Matthew 26:36–46.

1. As Jesus and the disciples walked to the Mount of Olives, he predicted that the disciples would abandon him (Mark 14:26–31), and that Peter would deny him. Why do you think he said these things?
2. By asking the three disciples to keep watch, what was Jesus really wanting from them?
3. What does the intimate term "Abba" indicate about Jesus' appeal to the Father?
4. Why did Jesus pray the same thing three times? Why would this not be vain repetition?
5. When he found the disciples sleeping, why did Jesus single out Peter?
6. What specifically might Jesus have meant by the "cup"? How is this an apt metaphor?
7. Knowing the inevitability of his death, why did Jesus bother praying?

8. What was the attitude of Jesus toward the disciples because of their sleeping? With what tone of voice did he admonish them?

9. What can we learn about praying and the will of God from this episode?

10. In your life, where does the statement about the spirit and the flesh prove true?

11. About which topics are you most intense in prayer?

The Arrest

Mark 14:43–52

Do you think I cannot call on my Father,
and he will at once put at my disposal
more than twelve legions of angels?
Matthew 26:53 NIV

Blessed are the merciful.

Maybe this chapter is misnamed even though the subtitles in many Bible versions refer to this passage as the arrest. Although an army of soldiers went to arrest him, and though he was completely innocent, in reality, Jesus turned himself in. Mark 14:42 indicates this as Jesus told his three sleepy friends, "Arise, let us be going; behold the one who betrays Me is at hand!" Obviously Jesus was not trying to escape nor hide.

We saw in the previous chapter that Jesus did not want to die. For him the cross meant suffering, shame, separation from God, and taking upon himself the sins of the world. He was young—in the prime of life—and he could still do so much good. But the Father's death sentence was irreversibly on him. God was sacrificing part of himself.

> *If only he could have died like a respectable martyr,*
> *hated by some, and mourned by others,*
> *but at least understood.*

Thoroughly Misunderstood

As painful as the crucifixion would be, Jesus also suffered much pain during his arrest. It is painful when we are misunderstood by everyone. Jesus had every reason to expect people to understand him because by this time he had been very open about his identity and mission. Nevertheless, we see in this passage great misunderstanding regarding Jesus by all who were involved in the passion events. No one really got a handle on the nature and identity of Jesus until after the resurrection.

If only he could have died like a respectable martyr, hated by some, and mourned by others, but at least understood. It would have been less painful emotionally. But he was thoroughly misunderstood. Some had false expectations for him. Others had deep suspicions of him. Why was Jesus so badly misunderstood? Mainly because people put their own needs ahead of God's kingdom. All the characters in this part of the story had their own agenda.

Judas—Murderous Motives

Notice, first, that Judas, the betrayer, expected Jesus to be a political hero. His agenda was selfish ambition. It is impossible to know Judas's exact motive. Was his primary concern for money? Was ethnic prejudice part of the problem? Maybe he was just greatly disappointed in Jesus and wanted to force his hand. We cannot know the exact motive of Judas, and maybe his motives were mixed. John's Gospel emphasizes Judas's financial greed, but the thirty pieces of silver Judas received was only the price of a slave—ten to twenty dollars. Judas certainly did not get rich by betraying Jesus.

Some suggest that Judas was a zealot, adamantly opposed to Roman occupation of Judea. In Jesus he saw someone who had the power and perhaps the reasons to expel the hated Gentiles. If so, Jesus disappointed him. Maybe Judas never expected the betrayal to result in the crucifixion. He thought he would force Jesus' hand,

and at the strategic moment Jesus would invoke supernatural power, overthrow the Gentile soldiers, and establish his kingdom.

Another idea is that Judas, an outsider, was jealous because others were closer to Jesus. The other eleven were Galileans. Judas's name indicates he may have come from Kerioth, a town in Judea. As an

> **Christianity has taken on the extreme cultural identity of being known as the religion of the West.**

outsider, it is possible he never felt that he belonged. Eventually his jealousy may have driven him to action.

Whatever his motive, he approached Jesus with the kiss of death. Judas identified Jesus to the soldiers by giving him the typical rabbinical greeting, though the language of the passage indicates a very intense kiss.

Judas represents for us those people who cannot distinguish between the kingdom of God and their own cultural aspirations. How tragic that Christianity has taken on the extreme cultural identity of being known as the religion of the West. This has happened for two reasons. First, those who are not of Western culture often see Christianity only as a Western religion, parallel to their own Eastern religions. This is ironic because, being Semitic, Jesus was much closer to being Oriental than Western. Nevertheless the clear intention was for the Good News of Jesus' coming to be taken into all the world so that every person of every cultural group would have a chance to hear and believe.

Second, Christianity is often identified as the religion of the West because many in this culture identify themselves as Christian simply because they were born into a so-called Christian nation. This often proves to be a great obstacle in witnessing. We need to contrast national citizenship with citizenship in God's kingdom. We need to help people understand that being born in the United States doesn't make one a Christian any more than being born in an oak tree makes one an acorn. Jesus clearly told Pilate, "My kingdom is not of this world" (John 18:36 NIV), thereby indicating that no earthly culture could claim to be Christian.

My friend, John Oostdyk, began a ministry in the Netherlands called "Atlantic Bridge." The purpose of the ministry is to enable young people from western Europe and North America to have cultural exchange experiences and to promote Christian teaching, particularly to Europeans who do not know the gospel. As we discussed his ministry, we observed that, ideally, cultural exchange needs to move in both directions. Thereby Europeans and Americans get to know each other's culture, but more importantly, people of both cultures exchange their culture for the kingdom of God. So it is with all people.

Judas represents for us a nationalistic perspective. He also represents a person who had espoused Jesus, only to betray him because of disappointment. Without doubt, every person who at one time has embraced Jesus and later abandoned him has started out with a wrong understanding of Jesus. Some seek in Jesus a respectable religious life. Others see him simply as a ticket to heaven. Still others want a perpetual religious high—an experience in which health, wealth, and prosperity are guaranteed. It is imperative that we know for sure Jesus' true identity. Otherwise, we will at some point be greatly disappointed because he does not meet our expectations.

The Jewish Authorities—Keeping the Status Quo

Jesus was also misunderstood by the Jewish authorities who considered him to be a blasphemous fraud. Their agenda was the status quo and Jesus was the threat. Therefore, they sent a delegation of chief priests, scribes, and elders, who comprised the three houses of the Sanhedrin. They went on an official arrest campaign, bringing with them an arsenal of support. Mark asserts that a multitude came with swords and clubs.

Their motive was to kill Jesus, which is why they needed to take him to the Romans. They considered him a fraud, especially his claims to be Messiah. In fairness to them, many false messiahs were on the scene during that time. Seneca, the Roman historian, mentions that all men were seeking *ad salutem;* seeking a savior or salvation.

Most Jewish people considered Jesus to be a prophet, albeit an unwelcomed one. The Jewish leaders considered him to be a threat because he undermined their authority in the eyes of the people. They sought the status quo because they wanted to retain their power and prestige.

Today people seem to be afraid to call Jesus a fraud; those who do not believe in him still maintain a profound respect for him. While most Americans probably do not believe Jesus truly is alive, few speak openly against him. They love to berate the church, but not its founder. However, if Jesus is not alive, and therefore not who he said he was, he was truly a great con artist and the fraud that the Jewish leaders considered him to be. He claimed to be the exclusive, unique Son of God, the Messiah—not a prophet, not a reformer, not a teacher of ethics. If he is not alive, then the Jews were correct: Jesus is a fraud.

Some people say that the New Testament writers made Jesus into the Messiah and Son of God through their writing. Such people do not believe the Scriptures were divinely inspired. They do not believe that we know what Jesus really said about himself. They do believe that he trained his disciples so they would perpetuate his memory and the movement he started by perpetrating the idea of his resurrection. If this is so, Jesus is all the more a fraud because he trained his disciples who wrote the Gospels. However, we must ask what was at stake for them to devise such a tale as the resurrection. People will die for a passionately held belief, but it is inconceivable that all eleven of the disciples would have died as persecuted martyrs for what they knew to be a hoax.

Today people can listen to the wonderful words about Jesus and the Good News of salvation and still be his enemy. This happened in the first century, and Jesus confronted the Jewish leaders by saying, "Every day I was with you in the temple teaching, and you did not seize Me" (Mark 14:49). Maybe they wanted to believe. Maybe people today want to believe. What inhibits them? In some cases it may be position, age, family, or religion. Maintaining the status quo means more to them than coming to a living relationship with the God of the universe through his Son, Jesus Christ.

The Roman Authorities—Protecting the State Religion

The Roman authorities also misunderstood Jesus. They expected him to be a rebel zealot. Their agenda was state religion and they were told Jesus was a fanatical rebel. Their only interest was in keeping the peace. Knowing Jesus' popularity, they saw this to be a situation fraught with danger; hence they brought weapons. Luke reported that a Roman cohort (six hundred soldiers) was sent to arrest Jesus. It is no wonder that Jesus asked, "Have you come out with swords and clubs as against a robber? While I was with you daily in the temple, you did not lay your hands on Me; but this hour and the power of darkness are yours" (Luke 22:52–53).

The Disciples—Safety First

We should not be surprised that Judas, the Jewish authorities, and the Roman authorities did not understand Jesus. We come now to the disciples. Surely they understood their master. Unfortunately, they did not know what to think. Their agenda at this time was safety. Earlier that evening all had vowed they would die before denying Jesus (Mark 14:31). But in the moment of truth they all fled. Their reason for forsaking Jesus was simple fear. With Jesus as their leader they were secure. He provided food, safety (such as from a fierce storm at sea), and a unique health insurance (his special healing touch). Now with Jesus arrested they feared for their safety.

A twentieth-century psychologist, Abraham Maslow, has developed a so-called pyramid of need in which he shows that the basic instinct of individuals is to seek to have physical needs (such as hunger) met first, then their safety needs, then their loving and belonging needs, then their self-esteem needs, and, finally, their self-actualizing needs. According to his thesis, the needs of the higher levels are not a concern until those of the lower levels are met. Therefore, physical needs must be met before safety needs, and safety needs before loving and belonging needs, and so on. An interesting study has shown that 70 percent of people who attend church do so to have safety needs met. Think about some of the most popular hymns of the church: "Rock of Ages," "Blessed Assurance," and "Leaning on the Everlasting Arms." These great hymns express wonderful truths while also appealing to our safety concerns.

Modern Christians are not all that different from the disciples. We also make a commitment to Christ in the safety of our group only to fall flat on our faces out in the world. Why? Fear. Fear of rejection by society, fear of being labeled a fanatic, fear of the loss of occupational advantages, fear of losing our family, fear of persecution—the list could go on and on. The disciples, however, had a better excuse than we do. They did not know how the story would end—that Jesus would rise from the dead and then send the Holy Spirit to be with them forever. We know Jesus is alive, and we have the Holy Spirit within us. We do not need to succumb to fear or be overly concerned about our safety needs. Maybe we need to remind ourselves more often that Jesus is always with us. Some of his last words were "Lo I am with you always, even to the end of the age" (Matt. 28:20).

The Young Man—Naked in the Garden

One other interesting character in the story may help further our understanding of different responses to Jesus. Only in Mark's Gospel do we meet the young man who was following Jesus and who was seized by the soldiers in the garden. He was wearing nothing but a linen sheet over his body. As he escaped, he left the linen sheet behind him and ran away naked.

Some biblical scholars suggest that this was young John Mark, the author of the Gospel of Mark. Who else would have known this occurred in the darkness of the night? Maybe this was Mark's way of putting his autograph on his own artwork. What were his reasons for following Jesus? Maybe he wanted to warn Jesus that the soldiers were coming. Perhaps he was following Jesus out of curiosity. If the upper room was in the home owned by his parents, he may have been eavesdropping on the Last Supper. When the disciples went out to the Mount of Olives, he followed.

Whatever his reasons, he showed great courage and real interest. Ultimately, however, he also fled. Many are curious about Jesus. They come close to deep identification with him but ultimately run. The symbolism is fascinating. Mark, running away naked, left Jesus. He reminds us of our first parents who, after realizing they were naked, hid in a garden. When we are without Jesus, we are spiritually naked. We need to be clothed in his righteousness.

Blessed Are the Merciful

Even though Jesus assured his enemies that he was not a military threat to them, they thought he might have been. They came with swords and clubs to arrest Jesus. Then Peter, in his zeal to defend Jesus and make good on his bravado, drew his sword and cut off the ear of the servant of the high priest. Jesus gently rebuked Peter, "Put your sword back into its place . . . do you think that I cannot

> **To be merciful is not only to feel others'
> pains and problems but also to extend relief.**

appeal to My Father, and He will at once put at My disposal more than twelve legions of angels?" (Matt. 26:52–53). Seventy-two thousand angels might have done a fair bit of damage to the six hundred foot soldiers! We must marvel at Jesus' restraint and mercy. Early on, during his temptations, Jesus had learned not to make improper use of his power when Satan had reminded him of angelic protection for the Messiah as promised in the Old Testament. What a temptation it must have been to use his power in the garden. Jewish leaders and Roman soldiers—their blood would make a fine stream down the Mount of Olives.

Was the mention of twelve legions of angels just Jesus' own brand of bravado? Or could he have done this? I do not think he was bluffing. Little did this valiant party of six hundred know they were at that moment experiencing mercy.

To be merciful is not only to feel others' pains and problems but also to extend relief. The follower of Jesus is quick to see pain, misery, and distress and looks for ways to bring healing, comfort, and help. To be merciful is to have compassion on others even when it is inconvenient to do so. Mercy, when it is shown, always overrides justice, giving better than what is deserved. If ever there was an inconvenient moment to show mercy, it was Jesus' arrest.

While the Romans misunderstood Jesus and thought him to be a fanatic with military power, at least they took his power seriously. Some people think of Jesus as merely an affable, benign character ready to go with anyone's agenda and accept the terms anyone offers. They are quite right in believing that Jesus is tolerant of many different external lifestyles. But he also demands an inward lifestyle that fanatically and radically projects the principles of the kingdom of God. Externally, Jesus was not eccentric. The soldiers would not have been able to identify him without Judas' kiss. Internally, he would soon demonstrate to them the character of the kingdom.

Christians often wonder how much we should conform to the culture around us. Jesus provided a perfect example. He was not an external nonconformist, that is, he did not seek to distance himself from the culture by appearance. He was an internal nonconformist, that is, he centered his affections and commitments on principles and a lifestyle based on the kingdom of God. This is not to say that externally we should seek to conform to the world, rather it suggests that external nonconformity is not necessarily a sign of piety. Unfortunately, in our day Christians often have it quite the reverse. We conform our inward values to worldly standards while externally our behavior distances us from the world, leaving us with no points of contact to reach the world with the gospel.

Your Agenda?

What would you have done in the garden that night? Like Judas, would selfish ambition cause you to be disillusioned with Jesus and betray him? Like the Jewish authorities, would desire for keeping the status quo cause you to view Jesus as a threat who needs to be disposed of? Like the Roman soldiers, would allegiance to a cultural religion cause you to help destroy him? Like the disciples, would concern for safety cause you to flee and abandon the master? Or perhaps like the young man described in Mark 14:51 (perhaps John Mark), are you out of curiosity so close, yet fleeing, spiritually naked?

However you respond, these questions may help indicate what you really believe about Jesus. In the next several chapters we will explore other responses to Jesus. Don't despair. Maybe you are not represented by one of the five groups we have just discussed. The important thing is that we understand fully who Jesus was, who he is, and how he wants us to relate to him. We want to come as close to him as we can, understanding him and growing deeper in our commitment to him. Surely as we draw closer we will find him to be a merciful master.

Group Study

Read Mark 14:43–52 and John 18:1–11.

1. John's Gospel records extended teaching and prayer by Jesus at the Last Supper (chapters 14–17). Look at John 17 and discuss briefly the prayer Jesus had just finished.
2. Discuss the treachery of Judas in Mark 14:10, 11, 18–21.

3. How does the soldiers' approach to Jesus show how little Judas understood his previous master? What do you think were Judas's intentions in betraying Jesus?
4. What elements in the account lead you to believe that it is the report of an eyewitness?
5. What special significance do you see in his response, "I am he" (cf., John 18:8)?
6. What is the cup that is referred to in John 18:11 (cf., Isa. 51:17, 22)?
7. How does the fact that Judas and Peter grossly misunderstood Jesus suggest that it is possible that even Christians today may not see Jesus from God's perspective? What advantages and disadvantages do we have?
8. How in this episode did Jesus personify "blessed are the merciful"? In what stressful situation might God be calling on you to show mercy?
9. How can we better understand the real mission and experience the real presence of Jesus?
10. Do you see any further meaning in "I am he . . . let these men go" in John 18:8? Has the arrest of Jesus (and subsequent death) let you go? From what?
11. Read (or sing) "Go to Dark Gethsemane."

> 1.Go to dark Gethsemane,
> Ye that feel the tempter's pow'r;
> Your Redeemer's conflict see;
> Watch with Him one bitter hour;
> Turn not from His griefs away;
> Learn of Jesus Christ to pray.
>
> 2.Follow to the judgment-hall;
> View the Lord of life arraigned.
> Oh, the wormwood and the gall!
> Oh, the pangs His soul sustained!
> Shun not suffering, shame, or loss;
> Learn of Him to bear the cross.
>
> 3.Calvary's mournful mountain climb;
> There, adoring at His feet,
> Mark that miracle of time,
> God's own sacrifice complete;
> "It is finished!" - hear the cry;
> Learn of Jesus Christ to die.
>
> 4.Early hasten to the tomb
> Where they laid His breathless clay;
> All is solitude and gloom.
> Who hath taken Him away?
> Christ is risen! He meets our eyes.
> Saviour, teach us so to rise. Amen.

12. Pray and thank Jesus for new insights and especially for his willingness to "drink the cup."

The Jewish Trial and Peter's Denial

● ● ● ● ● ○ ○ ○ ○ ○

Mark 14:53–72

"I am," said Jesus. "And you will see the Son of Man
sitting at the right hand of the Mighty One
and coming on the clouds of heaven."
Mark 14:62 NIV

Blessed are the pure in heart.

Late in the summer of 1992 our nation's eyes were riveted on the Senate confirmation hearing of Clarence Thomas to become a Supreme Court justice. The hearing became controversial when Ms. Anita Hill alleged that Judge Thomas had been guilty of sexually harassing her in a previous work-related situation. Because this was a confirmation hearing, all the trappings of a courtroom drama were present. In reality, two trials were occurring. On the one hand, Judge Clarence Thomas was on trial. His reputation was in jeopardy; his nomination to the Supreme Court would be confirmed or denied depending on the ruling of the Senate committee. On the other hand, another trial was occurring. American citizens, who normally had little awareness of and contact with United States senators, were

> ***The horror, shame, and humiliation
> of the last twelve hours of Jesus' life prior
> to his crucifixion are impossible to exaggerate.***

watching a committee of senators at work. Truly the senators were on trial in the minds of the American public.

In a sense every time a jury convenes to render judgment about a defendant, the defendant is not the only one on trial. The jury is also. Will the jury carry out justice, or be swayed by personalities, circumstantial evidence, and so forth?

Never was this more true than in the trials Jesus went through. We say trials because all four Gospels reveal that on Thursday night and Friday morning Jesus was forced six times to respond to the accusations against him. First, he was taken immediately after his arrest to the house of Annas, who at this time held no office. He had been high priest for many years, but more recently four of his sons had been high priests. Truly, he was the power behind the throne. Caiaphas, the present reigning high priest, was Annas's son-in-law. We will see in a moment why Jesus was taken to Annas. Second, he appeared before Caiaphas; the account recorded in Mark 14:53–72. He also appeared before the entire Sanhedrin, after which he was then led to Pilate, who questioned him briefly. Upon finding out that Jesus was a Galilean, Pilate forwarded him to Herod, who happened to be in Jerusalem at the time. Herod queried Jesus for a while but sent him back to Pilate for the final trial.

History stands in judgment on each of those trials. We will see the farcical charades of justice that took place. In the text, the plaintiff (some of the Jewish leaders) and the jurors (the Sanhedrin) appear to be most uncomfortable before the defendant (Jesus)—a defendant whom history will reveal to be the Judge of all mankind.

The horror, shame, and humiliation of the last twelve hours of Jesus' life prior to his crucifixion are impossible to exaggerate. His arrest in the garden probably occurred about nine o'clock in the evening. Between then and nine o'clock the next morning, Jesus endured the six trials mentioned above.

Trial by Error

The first trial was unofficial. Annas wanted Jesus to appear before him because he had been greatly irritated by a particular action of Jesus. Annas wanted to gloat over Jesus and, more or less, to have the last say. What had Jesus done that so angered the former high priest? In an act of righteous outrage, Jesus had driven out of the temple the money changers and those who sold pigeons and doves to worshippers wishing to make their offerings in the temple.

You may recall that the requirement for sacrifices was that the animals would be without spot or blemish. To ensure that this was the case, the temple had appointed inspectors to examine the animals. Most pilgrims coming to Jerusalem bought their sacrifices—pigeons, doves, and lambs—outside the temple and brought them in to be sacrificed. More often than not, the inspectors would find a flaw in those animals and suggest that the pilgrims buy their sacrifices in one of the stalls within the temple precincts, since those stalls had already been inspected and the animals judged to be acceptable. This was all fine and well except that outside the temple a person could buy two pigeons, for example, for about the equivalent of nine cents. Inside the temple the same two pigeons would cost a dollar fifty.

It was Annas who owned these temple stalls. In fact, they were actually called the bazaars of Annas. From this little industry, Annas and his family made the equivalent of $140,000 a year. Therefore, when he had the opportunity to gloat over the young Galilean who had interfered with his vested interest in the temple, Annas was eager to do so.

After appearing before Annas, Jesus was led to the home of Caiaphas, the present high priest. This examination, also not an official trial, was an investigation to drum up a charge to levy against Jesus before the Sanhedrin. This interview lasted for several hours until finally the charge of blasphemy was trumped up. Jesus would be accused of claiming to be the Son of God.

By this time it was early in the morning and Jesus was taken to the Sanhedrin, the Jewish supreme court of religious matters. The Sanhedrin had power to issue the death sentence, but because Palestine was under Roman jurisdiction, the Jews were not allowed to carry it out. To do that they needed Roman concurrence and participation.

The Sanhedrin existed not only to ensure religious propriety but also to protect each trial defendant. The constitution of the Sanhedrin ensured that every defendant would be given the benefit of the doubt, and in most cases it was a very lenient court.

Seventy people comprised the Sanhedrin with the high priest as its president. The courtroom was arranged in a semicircle so that members could see one another. When verdicts were handed down, they were given individually by all seventy, beginning with the youngest and moving toward the oldest. This guaranteed that there would be no undue influence by the veteran members. Evidence that was supported by two or more witnesses was the only evidence allowed, and then each piece of evidence had to be examined independently. One thing that was definitely outlawed was asking a question that would cause a defendant to incriminate himself. In the rare instances when a death verdict was given, the Sanhedrin did not allow the execution to be carried out the same day. A whole night had to elapse so that the Sanhedrin would have the opportunity to reconsider and, possibly, change the verdict or extend mercy.

That is how the Sanhedrin should have handled the case of Jesus. When we look at what actually happened, it is clear that there were no independent verdicts, that the high priest asked Jesus an incriminating question, and that a night elapsing between the verdict and the execution was not allowed. In other words, the Sanhedrin very uncharacteristically acted as a lynch mob, rushing to execute Jesus as quickly as possible.

Blessed Are the Pure in Heart

Mark's account of the fraudulent trial before Caiaphas and other members of the Sanhedrin shows an interesting juxtaposition between the sinful treachery of the accusers and the honest, self-revealing testimony of Jesus. My feelings as I read the trial narrative are ambiguous. I am frustrated; why didn't Jesus speak up and set the record straight? In chapter 1 we saw several attempts to make Jesus look foolish. Each time, he turned the tables and made the skeptics look foolish. Surely, he could have done that again. Why did he submit to this abuse?

Then, I admire Jesus. How majestic, how superior, how in control he appears. His silence says it all because he is the Word.

Why did Jesus subject himself to this dangerous nonsense? I believe it was because he was pure in heart. He had no need to hurt his abusers; he surely did not want to dignify their deceitful schemes by participating; he knew it was the Father's purpose for him to go to the cross, and he focused on that one thing.

To be pure in heart is to desire one thing. To be pure in heart is to have a simple, sincerely motivated will—no deviousness, no ulterior motives, and no baseness. The whole life, public and private, of the pure in heart is transparent before God and man. Hypocrisy and deceit are abhorrent; they are without guile.

The pure in heart are promised that they will see God. Knowing this, Jesus, "for the joy set before Him endured the cross, despising the shame, and has sat down at the right hand of the throne of God" (Heb. 12:2). His purity, his innocence, his regal bearing, his white-hot honesty, transcend the injustice of the trial. In his time of severest testing, Jesus' character did not change.

The accusers' treachery is heightened by several illegalities. The time for the trial was illegal, being held at night and during a great feast. By Jewish law both of these features should have ruled out the trial. The place of the trial was illegal. The Sanhedrin was supposed to meet in the Hall of Hewn Stone; this hearing was held in the house of Caiaphas.

More blatantly illegal than the time and the place was the fact that the chief priests and the whole Council, according to Mark 14:55, had already passed sentence upon Jesus. The trial was merely to obtain testimony to put Jesus to death, not to do justice. Therefore, they were seeking false testimony from various so-called witnesses. Even the false witnesses were not able to present a consistent story, finally forcing Caiaphas to take matters into his own hands. He asked Jesus an outright illegal, self-incriminating question: "Are you the Christ, the Son of the Blessed One?" (Mark 14:61 NIV).

Also illegal was the verdict, which should have been given by each member individually. Instead, the high priest interposed his own verdict, accusing Jesus of blasphemy and, therefore, deserving of death. Then, rather than allowing a night to elapse between sentence and execution, the mob held a final consultation a few hours

> *How odd that the most righteous man ever received such a fraudulent, prejudiced, bloodthirsty trial.*

later (still early in the morning), after which they bound Jesus and took him to Pilate.

One does not have to be a disciple of Jesus to notice how treacherous, how depraved, how perverted the chief priests, scribes, and the whole Sanhedrin acted in this charade of a trial. Consider the irony. Even from a legal, objective, nonsectarian point of view, it is odd that a man, acclaimed now for centuries by millions of people to have been the most holy and righteous man ever, could have received such a fraudulent, prejudiced, bloodthirsty trial. The behavior of the Jewish leaders was convincing testimony of the truth Jesus declared as recorded in John 3:19–20 (NIV):

> This is the verdict: Light has come into the world, but men loved darkness instead of light because their deeds were evil. Everyone who does evil hates the light, and will not come into the light for fear that his deeds will be exposed.

Trying Jesus Today

Let us bring our text a little closer to home and see if we can find in the responses to Jesus a bit of the twentieth century. The characters in the story illustrate how people put Jesus on trial and judge him today.

Indecision

Early in the text (14:54) Mark keeps us in touch with Peter, who followed Jesus at a distance right into the courtyard of the high priest, where, sitting with various servants, he was warming himself at a fire. Peter represents for us twentieth-century indecision. Imagine his confusion. Was Jesus really the conquering Messiah whom Peter had acclaimed at Caesarea-Philippi? Perhaps at this point Peter was agnostic. He did not know what to believe. While he wanted to believe Jesus was the Messiah, Peter may have been unsure at this point. In our day it's fashionable to be agnostic—a term that comes from two Greek words, *a* and *gnōsis* and means literally *no knowledge*. Some people believe that to be intellectually honest, one must not form an opinion on religious and nonscientific matters. Taking a stance on the identity of Christ is viewed to be intellectually presumptuous, since experimental proof of his identity is impossible. Remaining uncommitted is far easier and more respectable.

The problem with agnosticism, however, is that when one does not know whether to believe or not, one is really affirming a belief. Belief demands commitment, and everyone is committed to a worldview. Those who believe in God worship God. Those who do not believe or are unsure about what they believe do not worship God. There is no middle ground between worshipping God and not worshipping God. Does the alleged agnostic worship God every other day and not worship him in between simply to be faithful to his indecision? How preposterous! The confessing agnostic is in reality a practicing atheist because, in his indecision, he chooses not to worship God and thereby professes belief in no God.

An analogy to this is a bachelor who is agnostic about marriage. He makes no decision, declaring that marriage might be good or it might be bad. But in his indecision he remains a bachelor. To not marry is, by definition, to choose to be a bachelor. Agnosticism is a legitimate position temporarily, while one engages in honest inquiry. But eventually the agnostic must declare himself. Perpetual agnosticism is dishonest and hypocritical.

Insincerity

Another twentieth-century perspective is seen in the first witnesses, described in Mark 14:56. They represent insincerity and testify with a hidden agenda. They were chosen by the chief priests and full council, according to verse 55, in order to give false testimony. The Jewish leaders were using these false witnesses as pawns to facilitate their own self-centered purposes. We have already seen that Annas, for example, had a vested interest in doing away with Jesus to preserve his highly profitable business and comfortable lifestyle. Many people today know in advance that they do not want to believe in Christ because their own self-centered priorities would then need to be changed.

Unbalanced Truth

The second witnesses, described in Mark 14:57–59, represent inaccuracy. Purposefully they confused the facts. They claimed to have heard Jesus say, "I will destroy this temple made with hands, and in three days I will build another made without hands." Jesus never said he would destroy the temple. His statement in John 2:19 (NIV) was, "[If you] destroy this temple. . . ." and in Mark 13:2 (NIV), "Not one stone here will be left on another." Yes, Jesus did predict that the temple would be destroyed, and that did happen in 70 A.D. He never said, however, that he himself would destroy the temple.

Two contemporary groups come to mind who distort the facts and in their inaccuracy find an excuse not to believe Jesus. First are those who hold to liberal theology and separate the Jesus of history from the Christ of faith. They scour the New Testament seeking any shred of evidence to support their dichotomy. They do not want to be in the unfashionable posture of believing in anything miraculous such as a virgin birth or an incarnation. Their self-deceit is this: They already have their minds made up about the outcome prior to examining the facts of the New Testament.

The second group are the cults. They are individuals and groups who focus all their attention on one aspect of truth and ignore the balanced teaching of Scripture. The Greek word translated *heresy* literally means truth out of balance. To call someone a heretic is not to say that he or she is entirely wrong in every aspect of doctrine. Rather, it suggests that the person's views are incomplete because he or she focuses on one small piece of the picture. An example of this is the Jehovah's Witnesses, who claim that Colossians 1:15, which calls Jesus "the first-born of all creation," is evidence that Jesus did not preexist eternally within the Godhead but came into existence at the time of his birth on earth. Despite the overwhelming evidence of biblical teaching regarding the preexistence of Jesus, the Jehovah's Witnesses take this verse, misinterpret the meaning of the words, and develop a doctrine to their liking. Like the Sadducees, they are mistaken because they "do not understand the Scriptures, or the power of God" (Mark 12:24).

> *Unbelievers, rather than seeing us as a loving, wholesome, upbuilding alternative to a godless society, are seeing a nasty, negative, manipulating, self-serving group of intolerant religious fanatics.*

Anger and Insolence

Caiaphas and the other Sanhedrin members represent two common twentieth-century responses to religious truth—anger and insolence. Mark 14:63–65 tells how angry Caiaphas and the others became. Imagine these so-called men of God spitting at Jesus, slapping him, mocking and humiliating him, and treating him as a fool and a fraud with "righteous" indignation. They accused him of blasphemy. Imagine this wretched bunch of lawbreakers acting as guardians of the almighty God's interests.

Many in today's society, and their numbers continue to grow, are haters of Jesus. The early Christians had to learn how to respond lovingly to these enemies of the gospel, even while being persecuted. I suspect that today's generation of American Christians will face severe testing by the enemies of Christ.

Increasingly, because we consider America to be a Christian nation, evangelical Christians—often called the religious right—are lobbying, politicking, and protesting in a variety of ways to maintain an ethical agenda in a secular society. In doing so, however, we may distance ourselves from the very world that God sent his Son to die for. Unbelievers, rather than seeing us as a loving, wholesome, upbuilding alternative to a godless society, are seeing a nasty, negative, manipulating, self-serving group of intolerant religious fanatics. Why has this happened? The church seems to have taken on a worldview of demanding its rights, rather than lovingly presenting the positive message of the gospel.

The anger and insolence represented by Caiaphas and his group will continue to be the stance taken by the world against the Christian church. How we respond will either open doors of opportunity to present the true picture of Christ or slam those doors so that we will never have an opportunity to present the life-giving message of the gospel.

Sharply contrasted with the sinful treachery of men, we see in this text the honest, self-revealing testimony of Jesus. As he endures this mockery of a trial, we are first impressed by his silence. He appears calm and undisturbed, looking on Caiaphas with clear eyes. The silence grows more and more intense. To the false testimony and the questions of the Sanhedrin Jesus gives no reply. Finally in great exasperation, Caiaphas steps forward and says, "Do You make no answer? What is it that these men are testifying against You?" (Mark 14:60). Still he kept silent and made no answer.

Gradually it dawns on the Sanhedrin that this significant silence is really the answer to the hollow questions of the excited high priest. The weight of Jesus' silence grew in the ears of those present, shouting to the whole Council that the trial was a mockery and not worthy of Jesus' participation.

Finally, in total frustration, Caiaphas poses a very direct and unambiguous question. Everyone understood what he was asking, "Are You the Christ, the Son of the Blessed One?" (v. 61). In his piety Caiaphas used the common circumlocution for the name of God

> ## "Are you the Son of God?"
> ## That is still the question of the hour.

by calling him Blessed One. His question really was, "Are you the Son of God?" That is still the question of the hour.

We have already seen that asking a defendant a self-incriminating question was illegal. Nevertheless, for the sake of truth and honor, Jesus indulged Caiaphas with the answer he wanted to hear. His purity of heart elicited an honest answer to the illegal question—a decisive yes.

The Example of Peter

We move now from one man, Caiaphas, who was uncomfortable in the presence of Jesus' silence, and return to another man, Simon Peter, who was uncomfortable in the presence of people he wished would have remained silent. The study of Peter in Mark's Gospel is especially important because we now know that Peter was almost certainly Mark's source for writing the Gospel. Imagine Peter's great humility in telling the story. Repeatedly, Peter included incidents that put himself in a bad light.

Like all of us, Peter had his good days and bad days. This particular Thursday night/Friday morning of the Passion Week was bad. Let's rehearse the action and dialogue that had been occurring:

Last Supper
Jesus: "You will all fall away; I have prayed for you Peter."
Peter: "The others maybe, but not me."
Jesus: "You will deny me three times tonight."
Peter: "I'll die before I deny you."

Garden
Jesus: "Watch with me one hour."
Peter sleeps.
Jesus: "Keep watching and praying."
Peter sleeps.
Jesus: "The spirit is willing but the flesh is weak."
Peter sleeps.
Jesus: "Awake, let us go meet the betrayer."
Peter slices off the right ear of the servant.
Jesus: "Put away your sword."
Peter follows Jesus at a distance.

Courtyard
Servant girl: "You were with Jesus the Nazarene."
Peter: "What are you talking about?"
Maid: "This is one of them."
Peter denies it.
Bystanders: "You are one. Your Galilean accent gives you away."
Peter curses and swears.
Rooster crows.
Peter sees Jesus and weeps.

All this puts Peter in a very bad light, and remember, Peter himself gave Mark the information. Earlier we saw that Peter seemed confused, maybe even agnostic; but his intellectual honesty was winning out. His cursing as he denied knowing Jesus was an obvious overreaction.

Another way of looking at the events, however, is to see Peter's intense desire to be faithful to Jesus. We need to recognize that up to the very last moment Peter's behavior had been one of fantastically reckless courage. With a small sword he was ready to take on the whole garden mob by himself. After slicing off the ear of the high priest's servant, common sense should have urged Peter to head for the hills. Surely he should not go to the courtyard of the high priest's house. Yet that is precisely where he went. The others had fled; Peter was intent on keeping his word. He would stick with Jesus even to the end.

Unfortunately, he overestimated his courage. Sitting by the fire, probably wrapped in his cloak, Peter was unexpectedly recognized. Immediately he denied all connection with Jesus. Any less of a man would have escaped that potentially dangerous situation as quickly as possible. Not Peter. He stayed. A second time Peter was identified and again he denied Jesus, even swearing that he did not know him. After the third denial, the rooster crowed, and remembering his Lord's warning, Peter's heart broke.

As condemning as we might be of Peter, we do well to remember that he fell prey to a temptation that could only have come to a man of great courage. William Barclay states, "It ill becomes prudent and safety seeking little men to criticize Peter for falling to a temptation which would never in the same circumstances have come to them at all."[1]

Weaknesses We Share

Thus, we acknowledge Peter's greatness of spirit, but Peter himself would encourage us to look carefully at three weaknesses that hindered him and that might also upset even the best of our spiritual intentions.

Overconfidence

First, notice that Peter was overconfident. His statement, "Even though all may fall away, yet I will not" (Mark 14:29), set him up for the fall. Often in Christian circles we are encouraged to grow in our confidence. Surely a fine line exists between fearfulness or lack of faith on the one hand, and overconfidence on the other. Christians can and ought to be confident in their relationship with Jesus. I like to read the short epistle of 1 John whenever I am in need of greater confidence—verses like 5:11–12: "And the witness is this, that God has given us eternal life, and this life is in His Son. He who has the Son has the life."

Christians must not, however, be confident of their own strength. Perhaps this is where Peter stumbled. Not being able to stay awake in the garden should have tipped him off that he was not at his best. We are never at our best when we rely on our own strength. Paul wrote about those who commend themselves by measuring themselves strictly by human categories. He insisted that any confidence or boasting ought to be done in the Lord (2 Cor. 10:13–18). Human flesh is certainly not a source to rely on in the spiritual battle. I recall a teenager who objected to her father's strict curfew. She had a rather chummy boyfriend with whom she enjoyed being out at night. Discussing her very unfair 11 P.M. curfew, she said to her father, "You don't trust me." His response was very wise: "You are right. I don't trust you because I don't trust the flesh. Your flesh or my flesh. The spirit may be willing but the flesh is weak."

Ultimately a Christian's confidence ought to be in direct proportion to his dependence on God. Peter provided the perfect illustration of this in the episode of walking on the water. As he remained in direct dependence on and contact with the Lord, he overcame the elements and his lack of confidence. Taking his eyes off Jesus, however, his confidence and his body sank. Maybe that is why years later he wrote, "Humble yourselves, therefore, under the mighty hand of God" (1 Peter 5:6).

Insensitivity

Secondly, notice that Peter was insensitive. He slept when Jesus needed him, fought when Jesus didn't want him to, and denied Jesus when he needed to be the most strong. Sharpening spiritual sensitivity is an important goal for every Christian. We can do this by getting to know what God is like and what pleases him. That is why having a daily encounter with God in devotions, private worship, or quiet time is important. Passages like Micah 6:6–8 help us understand what pleases the Lord. Meditating on such passages helps us become spiritually sensitive.

We also sharpen our spiritual sensitivity by considering every event in life to be a spiritual opportunity. As we see God in the little things of our lives, we respond more sensitively to him. Soon after the crucifixion and resurrection of the Lord when the early church was being formed, Peter found himself eating with Gentiles. When Jewish-minded Christians approached, he recoiled from the fellowship with Gentiles. Paul confronted him, and this proved to be another lesson for Peter to learn. Had he seen the presence of God in the event, and had he been sensitive to the need to obey despite his fear about being criticized, Peter would have won that victory.

Perhaps more than any other way, we sharpen our spiritual sensitivity by wanting to be pure in heart. Jesus' saying, "The spirit is willing," ought to be utilized. We must affirm the Spirit within us. Dr. A. W. Tozer preached, "We all have as much of God as we want." His little booklet, *Five Vows for Spiritual Power,* focuses on gaining spiritual sensitivity. The five vows are: (1) deal thoroughly with sin, (2) never own anything, (3) never defend yourself, (4) never pass on anything about anybody that will hurt him, and (5) never accept any glory.[2]

Cowardice

Thirdly, Peter stumbled because, for that moment at least, he was cowardly. Despite all the things we said earlier about Peter's courage, at the moment of truth, he was a coward. Why did he deny Jesus? Why do we sometimes deny Jesus?

Peter feared persecution. Because of his association with Jesus, he could easily have been arrested. Years later, perhaps reflecting back on this terrible episode in his life, he warned fellow believers not to be taken off guard by fiery ordeals and testings that were occurring in their lives. The teaching he gave in 1 Peter 4:12–16 is extremely helpful to Christians who at times are cowardly.

Denying Jesus means being ashamed of him before men. No doubt Peter reflected in later years on what he helped Mark put in his

Gospel, "Whoever is ashamed of Me and My words in this adulterous and sinful generation, the Son of Man will also be ashamed of him when He comes in the glory of His Father with the holy angels" (Mark 8:38).

Fearing persecution and being ashamed of Jesus before men puts us in great danger. A commentator named Wescott wrote, "John, who remained closest to the Lord going on into the audience chamber, remained unmolested. Peter, who mingled with the indifferent crowd, fell."[3] The place of compromise is never the place for the Christian.

The short hymn "Jesus, and Shall It Ever Be" summarizes this lesson and Peter's experience.

> Jesus and shall it ever be,
> A mortal man ashamed of thee?
> Ashamed of thee whom angels praise,
> Whose glories shine through endless days?
>
> Ashamed of Jesus—that dear friend,
> On whom my hopes of heaven depend?
> No, when I blush, be this my shame—
> That I no more revere his name.
>
> Ashamed of Jesus? Yes, I may
> When I've no guilt to wash away,
> No tear to wipe, no good to crave,
> No fears to quell, no soul to save.
>
> Till then nor is my boasting vain.
> Till then I boast a Savior slain.
> And, oh, may this my glory be,
> That Christ is not ashamed of me.

Group Study

Read Mark 14:53–72 and John 18:12–27.

1. Read the parallel passages (Matt. 26:57–75 and Luke 22:54–71), and discuss any significant information not included by Mark and John.

2. Discuss Caiaphas's previous statement found in John 11:49–50. Was he being prophetic, sinister, or commanding?

3. What irony is suggested by the timing of Jesus' trial and Peter's denial?

4. Given the themes of the high priest's questions in John 18:19, what specifically do you think he may have asked Jesus? Why could not the witnesses mentioned in the other Gospels agree?

5. How would you characterize Jesus' admission of his identity? Was it suicidal? Necessary for honesty's sake? Braggadocio? Evangelistic? Why did Jesus divulge his identity so clearly?

6. How does the Gethsemane experience give us a clue to Peter's inconsistency at this point?

7. How can you as a Christian combat both the false evidence used by some people to discredit Christ and the ignorantly hostile attitude of others?

8. In identifying with Jesus, do you find yourself willing to submit passively to the injustices of a post-Christian, prejudiced society? (See John 15:18–16:4.) Should you?

9. Suggest various reasons why Peter may have been in the courtyard. Why was he unwilling to own up to his relationship with Jesus? What reasons are most likely to keep you from verbally identifying with Jesus?

10. What kinds of vested interests do people have today that inhibit them from pursuing truth and justice? Do any such interests keep you from realizing the full blessing of abandoned discipleship?

11. Practically, what can we do to counter the weakness of the flesh, even though our spirit might be willing? What might Peter have done differently?

12. Share with one another any testings you see on your horizon, and then pray for each other.

The Roman Trial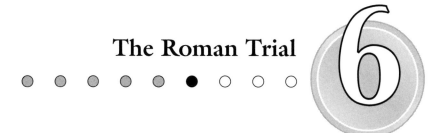

Mark 15:1–15

**But Jesus made no reply, not even to a single charge—
to the great amazement of the governor.**
Matthew 27:14 NIV

Blessed are the meek.

Humans throughout history have had a fascination with notorious characters. Idi Amin, Al Capone, Joseph Stalin, Adolf Hitler, Napoleon Bonaparte, Genghis Khan, Caesar Nero, and Nebuchadnezzar are but a few names of the antiheroes who intrigue students of history. No less an antihero is the man Pontius Pilate. Forever he lives in infamy because of the events we will consider in this chapter.

The Roman trial of Jesus presents two other parties whom we will consider. Besides Pilate, we see the mob of angry Jews and the prisoner Barabbas. Each of these parties faced a destiny-shaping decision. Pilate faced an existential dilemma—who, in reality, was this one so hated by the Jews? Was he really some kind of king? Why were they so threatened by him? The importance of Pilate's decision was not understood by even Pilate at the time, but he found it impossible to ignore the dilemma, pass it off onto someone else like Herod, or make an easy, convenient decision by ignoring the truth. He had to make a decision. He had to take a stand.

Members of the mob were confronted by a sociological dilemma. They belonged to a religious system that had prostituted itself to a

> *In the trial of Jesus, Pilate wanted to placate the Jews and yet exercise justice.*

secular political system. The selfish religious leaders were giving perverted direction to the people. Nevertheless, as they incited the mob to action, surely, it would seem, their motives were in the best interest of the nation. If the nation would be better with the Galilean rabbi dead, why should the members of the mob question the leaders?

Barabbas faced a theological dilemma. As a rebel against the government, Barabbas had been caught and declared guilty of murder. He was sentenced to be executed on a Roman cross. At the last minute, a pardon by the Roman governor was handed down and Barabbas was offered his freedom. Then he learned that a harmless Galilean teacher, who had become the object of jealousy of the religious leaders, had in a sense taken his place. How would Barabbas respond?

Pilate's Problems

Let us go back to Pontius Pilate, the leading character of this text. His official title was Procurator of the Province of Judea. He was responsible not to the Roman senate, but directly to the Roman emperor. Judea was known to be a province in constant turmoil because of the radical religious views held by many of the Jews. Pilate was contemptuous of the irrational prejudices of this strange group of people. In times past he had used an iron fist to rule, even though his predecessors had wisely dealt with the Jews with kid gloves. Pilate was not one to back down from Jewish pressure. When he led his Roman troops into Jerusalem, rather than removing the Roman standards that featured a little metal bust of the emperor, a symbol of his divinity, Pilate greatly offended the citizens of Jerusalem and defiled the city by bringing in these images of a false god.

Thousands of Jews protested and marched to Caesarea, Pilate's headquarters, begging him to stop violating their city in this way. The showdown eventually found Pilate backing down because the Jews were more than willing to be slaughtered to rid the city of the Roman flag. Even Pilate could not kill thousands in cold blood.

Soon after this incident, Pilate decided to build an aqueduct in Jerusalem and pay for it by taking money from the temple treasury. Naturally, a riot ensued, which Pilate intended to quell by dressing his troops in plain clothes and giving them clubs to carry under their cloaks. Pilate's intention was merely to beat up on the Jews a bit to stop the riot. The incident got out of hand; the soldiers lost control, and two thousand Jews were killed in the streets of Jerusalem.

This slaughter put Pilate in a bad light with the Roman emperor, who had ordered Pilate to treat the Jews gently. It also gave the Jews the upper hand because they could get Pilate in trouble by reporting any other examples of mismanagement. Therefore, in the trial of Jesus, Pilate was walking on eggshells, so to speak, wanting to placate the Jews and yet exercise justice. One thing is crystal clear from the trial account—Pilate was sure that Jesus did not deserve death.

Five Crucial Questions

In Mark's account, Pilate asked Jesus five questions that give insight into his judicial technique and his weakness of character.

Are You the King of the Jews?

The first question was, "Are you the king of the Jews?" (Mark 15:2 NIV). All four Gospels report this question. Undoubtedly Pilate had heard of Jesus and the claims that people were making. This question, however, came from the accusations being made against Jesus by the chief priests, scribes, and elders. Luke 23:2 reports the

Jews saying, "We found this man misleading our nation and forbidding to pay taxes to Caesar, and saying that He Himself is Christ, a King." Originally the Jewish leaders agreed on accusing Jesus of blasphemy, but knowing this would mean nothing to Pilate, they changed their tactic.

Jesus' answer to Pilate's first question is not all that clear. The Greek is not easily translated, although most translations give a positive reply. In reality his answer was, "So to speak" or, "In a manner of speaking." John's account (18:33–37) fills out this part of the dialogue in greater detail. Jesus went on to say, "My kingdom is not of this world." This confused Pilate and he replied, "So You are a king?" Jesus answered, "You say correctly that I am a king. For this I have been born, and for this I have come into the world, to bear witness to the truth" (v. 37). The key point here is that Pilate knew Jesus was not a political threat. Whatever the nature of his kingdom, it surely was not a rival to Rome. After this part of the examination, Pilate went out to the Jews and said, "I find no guilt in Him" (v. 38).

Throughout the encounter between Jesus and Pilate there is much irony. Here we find the King of Kings being asked if he is a king. His enigmatic answer veils the fact that he is not merely the King of the Jews, but indeed King of the universe. Pilate represents human rebellion by refusing to recognize true authority. The question each of us must answer is not merely, Is Jesus the King of the Jews? or, Is he the King of the universe? or, Is he the King of Kings?, but, Is he the King of me? Anything short of a positive answer leaves us all in the same position as Pilate.

Do You Make No Answer?

Pilate's second question was, "Do You make no answer [to their accusations]?" (Mark 15:4). After the initial interview, Pilate went out to the chief priests who gave further accusations against Jesus. Jesus heard these accusations but remained silent, causing Pilate to ask why he would not answer their charges. Their additional charges were: "He stirs up the people, teaching all over Judea, starting from Galilee, even as far as this place" (Luke 23:5). Jesus might easily and successfully have defended himself, but he chose the eloquence of silence.

Pilate, learning that Jesus taught in Galilee, asked whether he was a Galilean. Hearing a positive answer and knowing that Herod, the governor of Galilee, was in Jerusalem, Pilate sent Jesus to Herod for a hearing. Luke reports the trial before Herod and indicates that Jesus again remained silent. Herod and his soldiers treated Jesus with disdain and then sent him back to Pilate.

Blessed are the meek. We pause here to ask why Jesus chose not to defend himself. Certainly he did not have a death wish, so why did he not reply to the trumped-up charges? Most likely the reason is that Jesus knew that everyone involved in the plot already knew the truth.

> ### To be meek is to be gentle, mild, patient, and tenderhearted.

New information would not change their murderous intentions. Also, Jesus had already learned the blessedness of being meek. On many occasions Jesus could have used his unlimited power for his own advantage. Instead, he chose the way of gentleness.

To be meek is to be gentle, mild, patient, and tenderhearted. The word means *domesticated,* as of a wild animal being tamed for useful purposes. It involves a quiet, willing, cheerful obedience and submission to God that stands in direct contrast to the stubborn, willful rebellion and self-assertiveness of the natural man. It connotes not passiveness but active compliance.

We noted in the last chapter that one of the five principles for spiritual power listed by Dr. A. W. Tozer is not to defend oneself. This principle can be taken to an extreme that results in total passivity against evil forces. That was not what Tozer meant nor was it the basis for Jesus' remaining silent. A mark of spiritual maturity is the ability to allow our life and reputation to speak for us. When we become self-defensive, we express insecurity in God and in our own testimony.

Tozer tells about a godly man named Henry Suso whose reputation was being falsely maligned. Henry was being held up unjustly for public ridicule and scorn. One day while deliberating how he should respond to these attacks, he saw a small dog in his front yard playing with a doormat—grabbing it with his teeth, shaking it, tossing it into the air, and chasing it. Henry reported that this illustration was to him like the voice of God saying, "That mat is your reputation, and I am letting the dogs of sin tear your reputation to shreds and toss it all over the lawn for your own good. One of these days, things will change." Henry then gained peace in the situation and refused to defend himself.[1]

Do You Want Me to Release Him?

Pilate's third question was, "Do you want me to release for you the King of the Jews?" (Mark 15:9). At this point the questioning turns from Jesus to the mob. Pilate was certain that Jesus was innocent. Verse 10 says that he knew the chief priests had delivered up Jesus because of envy. While Pilate was seated on the judgment seat, his wife sent a note to him saying, "Have nothing to do with that righteous Man; for last night I suffered greatly in a dream because of Him" (Matt. 27:19).

Rather than answering Pilate, the chief priests stirred up the mob to ask for Barabbas to be released instead of Jesus. Pilate had reminded them that according to custom he had the prerogative to grant clemency to a criminal during Passover. He suggested that Jesus should be the one to receive that pardon. The mob, however, cried out saying, "Not this Man, but Barabbas" (John 18:40). Barabbas had been thrown into prison for committing murder during an insurrection. The irony here is evident. Jesus was being accused of being an insurrectionist, although no evidence supported that charge, while Barabbas, already a convicted insurrectionist and murderer, was requested to be released.

Pilate's decree was this:

> You brought this man to me as one who incites the people to rebellion, and behold, having examined Him before you, I have found no guilt in this man regarding the charges which you make against Him. No, nor has Herod, for he sent Him back to us; and behold, nothing deserving death has been done by Him. I will therefore punish Him and release Him.
>
> Luke 23:14–16

That was Pilate's intent. The Jewish leaders, however, incited a rowdy mob and began a chant for Jesus to be crucified and Barabbas to be released.

> *Like sharks frenzied from tasting a few drops of blood, they continued crying out, "Crucify, crucify!"*

What Shall I Do with Him?

Pilate's fourth question, also to the Jewish leaders, was, "Then what shall I do with Him whom you call the King of the Jews?" (Mark 15:12). Pilate could not believe the Jews would really demand the crucifixion of Jesus. But Pilate miscalculated the angry, murderous intent of the mob. All the more they cried out, "Crucify Him!" (v. 13). Pilate was surely in a dilemma. He knew their motives were wrong. He knew Jesus was innocent. The one position of possible compromise, using the Passover custom to release a prisoner, had backfired on him and now he had a bloodthirsty mob to mollify. Being the only one with the authority to execute capital punishment, Pilate was truly on the spot.

Why?

His final question was really a plea, hoping to find some measure of sanity and justice in the people. "Why, what evil has He done?" (Mark 15:14). Again, rather than answering, they continued with their chant, "Crucify Him!" (v. 14). Truly, the mob mentality had taken over.

Pilate then had Jesus scourged, a brutal whipping of thirty-nine lashes with a metal-laden whip that caused many prisoners to pass out and some nearly to die. The soldiers wove a crown of thorns and put it on Jesus' head, having clothed him in a purple robe. After taunting him as King of the Jews, the soldiers delivered Jesus back to Pilate who put this pitiful looking figure in front of the Jews, hoping to arouse their sympathy and find them satisfied with the harsh punishment already meted out. At that point Pilate admitted Jesus' innocence, "Behold, I am bringing Him out to you, that you may know that I find no guilt in Him" (John 19:4).

Far from being satisfied, the chief priests and officers, like sharks frenzied from tasting a few drops of blood, continued crying out, "Crucify, crucify!" (v. 6). Pilate responded saying, "Take Him yourselves, and crucify Him, for I find no guilt in Him" (v. 6).

Once more Pilate questioned Jesus about his identity, and when Jesus refused to reply, Pilate warned Jesus about his authority to release him or crucify him. Jesus responded, saying Pilate had no authority except what had been given from above. Again Pilate tried to release Jesus, but the Jews cried out, "If you release this Man, you are no friend of Caesar; everyone who makes himself out to be a king opposes Caesar" (John 19:12).

Caesar, King of the Jews

Charles Colson, in his book *The Body,* observes that Pilate had earlier been inducted into an elite group known as "Friends of Caesar."[2] This gave Pilate tremendous political leverage and potential. So, when the Jews accused him of not being a friend of Caesar if he allowed Jesus to escape, Pilate felt trapped. On the one hand, he did not want to succumb to the Jews in this charade of an accusation, but on the other hand he surely did not want to lose his status with Caesar. If he had to choose for either this innocent Jewish rabbi or Caesar, there was no contest. He brought Jesus out and said to the Jews, "Behold, your King!" (John 19:14). The Jews continued their chant, "Away with Him, away with Him, crucify Him!" (v. 15). Pilate, according to John's Gospel, asked, "Shall I crucify your King?" The chief priests answered, "We have no king but Caesar" (v. 15).

Do not fail to catch the significance of this last statement. The Jews historically had resolutely refused Gentile dominance and time and again had experienced the wonderful salvation and deliverance of God from foreign oppression. But these leaders, who called themselves "separated ones," out of total political treachery and expediency, now confessed that their only king was a Roman emperor. With that statement, all previous Jewish history stands in condemnation of them.

At this point, perhaps to assuage his own conscience, Pilate, according to Matthew's account, called for a basin of water and publicly

> *The issue is not whether we will wager,*
> *but how we will wager.*

washed his hands saying, "I am innocent of this Man's blood; see to that yourselves" (Matt. 27:24). The Jews responded saying, "His blood be on us and our children!" (v. 25). Tradition tells us that Pilate went insane trying to get the blood off of his hands. Even while publicly renouncing all responsibility for the unjust execution of Jesus, Pilate is viewed by history as the man who put Jesus to death.

Wager You Must

Reconsider Pilate's last question. It is foolish for one individual to ask others, "What shall I do with Jesus?" That is the most important question anyone can ever consider. And no one can give anyone else the answer. Each person must make that decision for himself or herself.

Many, like Pilate, try to avoid making a decision, but there is no escape. Sixteenth-century philosopher and mathematician Blaise Pascal is known for his "wager." Using the imagery of gambling, he made a point about Christianity. Pascal asserted that by being alive, we are already in the game. We must wager. The issue is not whether we will wager, but how we will wager. Pascal's contention is that since we do not have empirical evidence available, any wager we make is a step of faith. Everyone lives by faith. Pascal shows that if we wager our lives that Christianity is true, we stand to gain eternal salvation if we are right and lose nothing if we are wrong. If we wager that Christianity is not true, we stand to gain little if we are right and to gain eternal damnation if we are wrong. Pascal then drives home the point that only a foolish gambler would bet his life against Christianity. "So wager wisely," he says, "but wager you must."[3]

The Jewish Mob

While Pilate was certainly the central figure, aside from Jesus, during the Roman trial, the Jewish mob also has lessons to teach us.

Clearly the mob was under the control of the chief priests, scribes, and elders. We do not know any of the individuals in the mob, nor do we know whether they had been part of the story earlier. Some preachers point out the fickleness of the crowd that a week earlier had hailed Jesus as the King, calling out, "Hosanna" as they ushered him into the city of Jerusalem on that first Palm Sunday. Supposedly, these same people appeared at the trial to condemn Jesus as a criminal, taking up the chant, "Crucify him!"

Perhaps some people participated in both events, but the Good Friday mob was almost certainly a different group than the Palm Sunday crowd. Most of the people at the trial were a mixture of Jewish religious leaders and their deputized hooligans who became a lynch mob. Other folks who were there just did not know what to make of all the commotion. When the chant started up and they heard their religious leaders yelling, "Crucify him!" no doubt the spirit of the mob seized them and before long they, too, were yelling.

Maybe we see ourselves in the mob; generally 99 percent of us are deeply influenced by peer pressure, and one thing a mob will not condone is individuals thinking on their own. The irrational conduct of the crowd, reported in Mark 15:14, is seen in their refusal

Have you ever had to own up to your belief in Jesus in the midst of a non-Christian crowd?

to answer Pilate, who asked, "What evil has He done?" Their reply was merely more shouting.

Have you ever had to own up to your belief in Jesus in the midst of a non-Christian crowd? What about in a hostile, unbelieving crowd? On a few occasions I have found myself in that position and tasted slightly how peer pressure can erode courage. If Peter, who earlier expressed great courage in wanting to defend Jesus, could bow to the peer pressure of a few maidens, surely less committed people were unlikely to stand up against the peer pressure of the Jewish religious leaders.

Learning to stand alone against social pressure is one of the most difficult and important lessons for the follower of Jesus. Early Christians succeeded, but many of them paid for their devotion with their blood. Perhaps that is why the Greek word for witness is *martyr.* Many of the early believers gave witness to their faith and became martyrs.

Escaped Convict

Although undoubtedly unaware of all the activities surrounding Jesus, another significant character is Barabbas, who is unknown in the Gospels until we get to this point of the story. He was not, however, unknown to the Jerusalem citizenry. In fact, he was a notorious insurrectionist, accused and convicted of murder.

On death row Barabbas was the sinner who got off scot-free, the recipient of grace. Someone else died in his place, and he was given a new lease on life. All of us are represented by Barabbas. Some are still on death row, not having yet accepted Christ as the substitute. Certainly this was an option for Barabbas. When news came to him that the governor was going to free him, Barabbas could have rejected the pardon, as unlikely as that would have been. Millions today are doing just that. The price for their sin has been paid; the pardon has been offered, and yet they reject it. In such cases, condemnation continues until grace has been accepted.

Others have allowed Christ to be their substitute and his sacrifice to be applied to their lives. They have been set free. Nevertheless, they live aware that they owe a great debt of love. We do not know the sequel to Barabbas's story. Conjectures have been made that he became a believer in Christ, though we are not sure. Obviously he received a new lease on life, and whether or not he fulfilled his debt of love, he certainly owed much.

All who have received God's grace and have been pardoned for their sinfulness owe the same great debt. Perhaps the hymn writer Isaac Watts had this in mind when he penned "When I Survey the Wondrous Cross."

> Were the whole realm of nature mine,
> That were a present far too small.
> Love so amazing, so divine,
> Demands my soul, my life, my all.

Group Study

Read Mark 15:1–15 and John 18:28–40.

1. What was the terrible hypocrisy of the Jewish religious leaders in John 18:28? Suggest some examples from our society where a ritual is maintained while at the same time gross sinfulness is being practiced.
2. What evidences in the dialogues between Pilate and the Jewish leaders reveal this tension? (See John 18:29–32 and 19:6, 12-16, 20–22.)
3. After his discussion with Jesus in John 18:33–38, what understanding do you think Pilate had of Jesus? Did Jesus say enough for Pilate to make a "saving faith" response?

Read John 19:1–16.

4. Why do you think Pilate was more afraid when the Jews revealed their real motive for wanting Jesus crucified?
5. Do you see any special significance to the day on which this happened? If so, what?
6. What does the response of the chief priests to Pilate's question, "Shall I crucify your King?" indicate about them?
7. Was Pilate a victim of a tough moment of history, or should he be held responsible for killing Jesus? If Pilate was a victim, do others have legitimate excuses for rejecting Jesus?
8. Which verses in this section illustrate the meekness of Jesus?
9. In this narrative, do you see yourself in the position of:

   • Pilate—wanting to side with Jesus but bending to pressure from others?
   • The Jews—letting religion interfere with knowing Jesus?
   • Barabbas—escaping damnation because Jesus was found guilty?

   How does this make you feel?
10. Does the fear of others or loss of position or prestige ever cause you not to want to side with Jesus? Tell about a time

when this happened and its outcome, whether positive or negative.

11. Who was really on trial in this narrative? What are the dangers in continually trying to avoid making a decision about Jesus Christ?

12. Write a short paragraph relating what you think might have become of Barabbas after his release. How do you think he felt about Jesus? How do you identify with him?

The Crucifixion

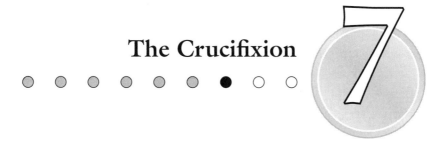

Mark 15:16–37

And when they had mocked him, they took off the
purple robe and put his own clothes on him.
Then they led him out to crucify him.

Mark 15:20 NIV

**Blessed are those who are persecuted
because of righteousness.**

Up to this point in our study of the Passion Week, the suffering of Jesus has been mostly psychological, spiritual, and emotional. He was misunderstood by the masses, maligned by the religious leaders, and abandoned by his closest friends. A shadow of sin,
death, and separation from the Father clouded his soul. The sham
of a trumped-up, false trial grieved his spirit. Jesus was also subjected
to a very painful scourging, which we have already discussed.

In this chapter we follow Jesus into the courtyard of Pilate to be
prepared for crucifixion, through the streets of Jerusalem bearing

the cross, and to Golgotha, the place of his execution. The physical pain Jesus would endure during this time cannot adequately be described.

> **Christ, the Lion of Judah, appeared
> before his tormentors as the Lamb of God.**

Even though we have divided the passion narrative into several episodes from the events in the upper room, to Gethsemane, to the house of Annas, to the palace of Caiaphas, to the court of Pilate, to the house of Herod, back to Pilate, into the Praetorium, through the streets of Jerusalem, and to Golgotha, all these episodes encompass less than twelve hours. The process was being rushed because the Jews wanted to be sure they would be holy and spiritually prepared for the Passover, which would begin that evening. Their original plan was to wait until after the feast before executing Jesus, but the timeliness of Judas' traitorous offer was too good to pass up. Little did the Jewish leaders know that they were on God's timetable, which would render the Passover celebration meaningless that year and for every year to come.

Blessed Are Those Who Are Persecuted Because of Righteousness

The crucifixion of Jesus is downright depressing. Like the Jewish pilgrims going to Passover, we would rather pass it by. But Jesus told his disciples to keep remembering his death. That becomes a bit easier when we remember that for those who are persecuted for the sake of righteousness, theirs is the kingdom of God.

Regardless of the kind of abuse Jesus suffered—physical, mental, emotional—one thing is certain: He was persecuted because of righteousness. His innocence was total and beyond question. Had Jesus not been morally and spiritually perfect, the religious leaders would not have resented him. His purity convicted them of their impurity and hypocrisy, so they persecuted him.

To be persecuted for the sake of righteousness is to suffer personal indignity, ostracism, and physical pain at the hands of those who cannot tolerate your example and reminders of righteous conduct. The blessedness of this rejection comes by knowing you are on the side of truth, and that you have borne a faithful witness.

More Meekness

Up to his crucifixion Jesus remained passive to the abuse he was suffering. In the last chapter we watched with wonder as Jesus perfectly exemplified the beatitude "Blessed are the meek (gentle)." Here, again, in a time of maximum stress Jesus remains in control. It is unfortunate that meekness is often taken to be weakness. The Greek word refers to strength under control. A powerful animal that has been tamed for domestic purposes is a good example. At a circus, we see in the center ring a cage with "wild" lions and tigers menacingly obeying their tamer/trainer. Their feigned threats are staged to enhance the thrill for the audience. In reality, these animals are the picture of meekness. Their strength and potential ferocity remain, but their spirits have been tamed and their actions trained.

Christ, the Lion of Judah, appeared before his tormentors as the Lamb of God; not only spotless and pure, but gentle and harmless. As Isaiah prophesied,

> He was oppressed and He was afflicted,
> Yet He did not open His mouth;
> Like a lamb that is led to slaughter,
> And like a sheep that is silent before its shearers,
> So He did not open His mouth.
>
> Isaiah 53:7

In great contrast to the passivity of Jesus throughout the mockery and crucifixion proceedings, notice the aggressive activity of the Roman soldiers. Mark 15:16–24 is filled with active verbs. They:

- took him away
- dressed him in purple
- wove a crown of thorns; put it on him

- acclaimed him, "Hail, King of the Jews!"
- beat his head with a reed
- spit at him
- knelt and bowed before him
- mocked him
- took the purple off him and put his garments on him
- led him out to be crucified
- pressed a passerby into service
- took him to Golgotha
- crucified him

Only God's Son could have meekly endured all that and at the same time loved his enemies. Let us look more closely at his passivity to the abuse against him.

Passive to Mockery

Jesus was passive in the face of mockery. Mark 15:16–20 shows the cruel mockery of the soldiers. Verses 29–32 describe the mock-

> *How would the world ever understand the kingdom of God when the King himself was subject to such ridicule?*

ery of people walking by and especially of the chief priests and scribes. Some of those passing by abused him and taunted him about destroying the temple and rebuilding it in three days. Others called out to him to save himself and come down from the cross. The chief priests and scribes taunted, "He saved others; He cannot save Himself" (v. 31). Verse 32 also indicates that those crucified with him were insulting him with the same mockery.

The taunting of those passing by may not have been malicious. They thought they were merely making sport of a poor, deluded Galilean. Nevertheless, it was painful for Jesus because he knew that the death he was experiencing was their only hope for salvation. Already Jesus was bruised and bleeding from the scourging, and perhaps, if his pain did not prohibit it, he was reflecting on the pitiful mockery of the soldiers that came from their misunderstanding of the nature of his kingdom. How would the world ever understand the kingdom of God when the King himself was subject to such

> **No one knows where his disciples were,
> but an unknown visitor is honored by God
> to bear the cross of Jesus.**

ridicule? Maybe he pondered the irony of the mockery of the Jewish leaders, "Let this Christ, the King of Israel, now come down from the cross, so that we may see and believe" (Mark 15:32). Jesus knew that in disobedience to the Father he could come down from the cross. He also knew that if he did, there would be nothing worth believing in.

Reading the crucifixion account, I must confess that I get more worked up over the mockery than over the crucifixion itself. The death of Jesus was a necessary part of God's plan, but the mockery was totally unnecessary. As I think of Jesus, standing with bloody pieces of flesh hanging from his tortured body, enduring the scoffing of ignorant, irreverent pagans . . . as I think of him wearing an old, faded purple cloak, blood running down his face from a crown of sharp thorns . . . as I think of him holding a swamp reed as a scepter and then of someone grabbing it to beat him until others also started pummeling his body . . . as I think of him being spat upon in mockery of the kiss of homage due royalty, I can hardly wait for him to come to vindicate himself so that every knee will bow and every tongue will confess that he is indeed King.

Max Lucado, in his magnificent book, *No Wonder They Call Him the Savior*, shows this same outrage. "Of all the scenes around the cross, this one angers me the most. What kind of people, I ask myself, would mock a dying man? Who would be so base as to pour the salt of scorn upon open wounds? How low and perverted to sneer at one who is laced with pain! Who would make fun of a person who is in an electric chair? Or who would point and laugh at a criminal who has a hangman's noose around his neck?"[1]

Modern-day criminals, even the most vicious serial killers, are given more dignity in death than Jesus experienced. The inhumane treatment he suffered would not be tolerated in today's legal system. Nevertheless, the mockery against his people and his church—the abuse Christians now and in the future will suffer—is in reality merely the ongoing sorrows of the Son of Man. To all this shameful treatment from Roman soldiers, Passover pilgrims, Jewish religious leaders, and crucified companions, Jesus was passive.

Passive to Intended Mercy

Jesus was also passive to the few expressions of intended mercy. Today you can go to the old part of Jerusalem and trace the stages of the cross along the Via Dolorosa. Each stage is greatly venerated by Christian pilgrims. When Jesus walked that way, he began by carrying the cross on his bloody back until, totally exhausted and depleted of strength, he was relieved of the cross.

The Roman soldiers, more out of hurry than compassion, grabbed hold of Simon of Cyrene, probably a black man, and put the cross-beam on his back. Isn't it interesting that Jesus had told his followers that to be a disciple one needed to bear his cross. At this point in the story no one knew where Jesus' disciples were, but an unknown visitor to Jerusalem was humiliated by the Romans and honored by God to be the one to bear the cross of Jesus.

Simon was probably a proselyte to Judaism who may have saved his money for years to attend a Passover in Jerusalem. Now he was enduring this shameful humiliation. Was he bitter? Angry at the Romans? Angry at this unknown criminal who could not even carry his own cross? No doubt his intention was to drop the cross as soon as possible and make his exit. But maybe not. Simon may have been fascinated by Jesus and perhaps even stayed around to watch him die. Did he become a believer? Most likely he did. Otherwise, why would Mark identify him so carefully as "the father of Alexander and Rufus" (15:21 NIV)? Many Bible scholars identify the same Rufus in Romans 16:13. Some suggest that Simon is the same man identified in Acts 13:1 as one of the teachers at Antioch, perhaps like Lucius "of Cyrene." If so, he continued to bear the cross of Jesus long after he dropped it on Golgotha. No words were uttered between Simon and

Jesus. Yet how reasonable that God would have chosen the one who literally bore the cross of Jesus to become a disciple.

Jesus was passive to another act of mercy described in verse 23. Proverbs 31:6 admonishes, "Give strong drink to him who is perishing. . . ." Often rich women of Jerusalem would perform this humane deed, thus drugging the victim and relieving his pain. Jesus refused the wine mixed with myrrh, choosing to die with his mind unclouded and fully aware of his mission. If ever in history anyone had an excuse to escape the problems and pain of life, Jesus surely did at this moment. Maybe today's "escape artists"—those who use drugs and alcohol—could learn from the Lord here. In all of Mark chapter 15 the only active thing Jesus did was to not take the drink.

Passive to Misunderstanding

Mark 15:29–32 shows that Jesus was also passive to the misunderstanding of the people. As the passion narrative moves along, we get upset with all the injustice, but when we arrive at verses 29–32, our anger rises sharply. The taunting, evil reveling, and verbal abuse are the height of cruelty; they are salt in the wounds, hitting a man when he is down. But the cruelty is due to a misunderstanding that

> **Needing to see in order to believe is like needing to acquire something in order to hope for it.**

people had all along. During the trial, Jesus was misrepresented as one who would destroy the temple and raise it in three days. Here again on the cross he hears the same misrepresentation turned into mockery. Jesus did not try to clear the misunderstanding or defend himself. Furthermore, he remained quiet while the Jewish leaders taunted him for not saving himself even though he saved others. A little theological lecture would have been most appropriate, but in meekness he refrained.

Perhaps the most difficult taunting to allow to go unchecked was their comment that he should come down from the cross and then they would believe. Would they have really believed? Jesus had said earlier, "If they do not listen to Moses and the Prophets, neither will they be persuaded if someone rises from the dead" (Luke 16:31).

The comment of the chief priests and scribes reveals an interesting relationship between the words *see* and *believe*. The Jewish leaders wanted to see in order that they might believe. Little did they understand their own contradiction. Needing to see in order to believe is like needing to acquire something in order to hope for it. If you already have it, you don't need to hope. Jesus told Thomas in John 20:29 (NIV), "Because you have seen me, you have believed; blessed are those who have not seen and yet have believed." Paul told the Romans, "For in hope we have been saved, but hope that is seen is not hope; for why does one also hope for what he sees?" (Rom. 8:24).

Another paradox is seen in the comments of the Jewish leaders. Notice their arrogance in asking the Son of God to come to them on their terms before they would believe. If he had done that, they would have exacted obedience from him, which is precisely the reverse of the way the relationship should be.

General Booth, founder of the Salvation Army, stated, "It is precisely because Jesus did not come down from the cross that we believe."[2] The cross expresses limitless love. Because Jesus went the whole way and died on the cross, we know that there is literally no limit to the love of God—nothing in all the universe that God's love will not endure if it reestablishes fellowship with humanity. Jesus was willing to endure passively the cruel misunderstanding of his enemies so that he could be the salvation of all.

Passive to the Murderous Act

Jesus was also passive to the murderous act conspired by both Romans and Jews. He was "obedient unto death, even the death of the cross" (Phil. 2:8 KJV). Purposefully we refer to the crucifixion as a murder. It was not an execution but a mob-ruled murder. While Romans and Jews conspired to perform it, many more share the responsibility. Dare we blame the Jews? Dare we blame the Romans? In truth, Adam and all his children are responsible for the crucifixion of Jesus. Paul Little affirmed this by saying, "Each of us, by doing as Adam did, has ratified the decision . . . to rebel."[3]

Up to this point we have mercifully refrained from describing the physical details of crucifixion. We have looked at the emotional, psychological, spiritual, and physical suffering that Jesus endured and his meekness in the face of it. While not wanting to be overly macabre, let us remind ourselves of the physical aspects of the death of Jesus to understand more fully the sacrifice that was required for Jesus to remain passive in the face of this murderous act.

After Simon dropped the crossbeam, long spikes were hammered between the two largest bones in Jesus' wrists into the wood. His feet were tied together. The crossbeams and Jesus were lifted to a vertical beam already in the ground. Jesus' feet were nailed together to the vertical beam with another spike. A hornlike rod projected from the vertical beam that, when straddled, allowed the victim to occasionally change the focus of pain from one part of his body to another.

Hanging there, suspended between heaven and earth, was a living body—breathing, seeing, hearing, feeling—reduced to a corpse-like state. Because of forced immobility and absolute helplessness, Jesus was not even able to writhe in agony. He was virtually unable to move. He had been stripped of his clothing, and he was unable to brush away the flies feasting on his lacerated body. He was exposed to the insults and cursing of people who delighted in the torture of others. Usually death was long in coming. One writer called it the acme of the torturer's act.

Dr. C. Truman Davis, a medical doctor, carefully researched the topic of crucifixion and wrote an article entitled "The Crucifixion of Jesus; the Passion of Christ from a Medical Point of View." His expression of the crucifixion is most moving.

Simon is ordered to place the patibulum on the ground and Jesus is quickly thrown backward with His shoulders against the wood. The legionnaire feels for the depression at the front of the wrist. He drives a heavy, square, wrought-iron nail through the wrist and deep into the wood. Quickly, he moves to the other side and repeats the action, being careful not to pull the arms too tightly, but to allow some flexion and movement. The patibulum is then lifted in place at the top of the stipes and the titulus reading "Jesus of Nazareth, King of the Jews" is nailed in place.

The left foot is pressed backward against the right foot, and with both feet extended, toes down, a nail is driven through the arch of each, leaving the knees moderately flexed. The Victim is now crucified. As He slowly sags down with more weight on the nails in the wrists, excruciating, fiery pain shoots along the fingers and up the arms to explode in the brain—the nails in the wrists are putting pressure on the median nerves. As He pushes Himself upward to avoid this stretching torment, He places His full weight on the nail through His feet. Again there is the searing agony of the nail tearing through the nerves between the metatarsal bones of the feet.

At this point, another phenomenon occurs. As the arms fatigue, great waves of cramps sweep over the muscles, knotting them in deep, relentless, throbbing pain. With these cramps comes the inability to push Himself upward. Hanging by His arms, the pectoral muscles are paralyzed and the intercostal muscles are unable to act. Air can be drawn into the lungs, but cannot be exhaled. Jesus fights to raise Himself in order to get even one short breath. Finally, carbon dioxide builds up in the lungs and in the blood stream and the cramps partially subside. Spasmodically, He is able to push Himself upward to exhale and bring in the life-giving oxygen.

Hours of this limitless pain, cycles of twisting, joint-rending cramps, intermittent partial asphyxiation, searing pain as tissue is torn from His lacerated back as He moves up and down against the rough timber: Then another agony begins. A deep crushing pain deep in the chest as the pericardium slowly fills with serum and begins to compress the heart.

It is now almost over—the loss of tissue fluids has reached a critical level—the compressed heart is struggling to pump heavy, thick, sluggish blood into the tissues—the tortured lungs are making a frantic effort to gasp in small gulps of air. The markedly dehydrated tissues send their flood of stimuli to the brain.[4]

In the case of Jesus, who died after only six hours, heart failure seems to have been the literal physical cause of death. John reports that the Jews, wanting to hurry the deaths so that they might prepare for Passover, asked Pilate to have the victims' legs broken, which would prohibit them from raising up to inhale and would soon suffocate them. When they came to Jesus, the soldiers noticed that he was already dead. One of the soldiers "pierced His side with a spear, and immediately there came out blood and water." John affirmed that he personally saw this occur (John 19:31–35). Dr. Davis also gave his insight regarding the cause of death inferred from the description in John 19:34 of the spear thrust in Jesus' side:

> And immediately there was an escape of watery fluid from the sac surrounding the heart and blood from the interior of the heart. We, therefore, have rather conclusive post-mortem evidence that Our Lord died, not the usual crucifixion death by suffocation, but of heart failure due to shock and constriction of the heart by fluid in the pericardium.

John adds that "he knows that he is telling the truth, so that you also may believe" (v. 35). In summing up his entire Gospel he wrote, "These [things] have been written that you may believe that Jesus is the Christ, the Son of God; and that believing you may have life in His name" (John 20:31). We who believe, believe that what was written was witnessed by John and the other disciples. Hopefully, the Roman soldiers, the Jewish pilgrims who passed by Golgotha, and even the Jewish leaders were able someday to read what was written and put their belief in the One whom they so shamefully mocked, the One who remained passive to their abuse.

Group Study

Read Mark 15:16–37 and John 19:17–30.

1. Divide into two groups, with one group taking Matthew 27:32–56 and the other taking Luke 23:26–49. Both groups should then report all the new facts given in their Scripture section.
2. Read Psalm 22:1–18 in unison. Find the references fulfilled in the Gospels that are predicted in this messianic psalm (see vv. 1, 7–8, 14–18).
3. What do you know about the physical aspects of crucifixion? Suggest some of the psychological and spiritual anguish that accompanied the physical pain of Jesus.
4. How does the verbal abuse of the chief priests, scribes, and elders show they thoroughly misunderstood messiahship?

How was this challenge like other temptations in Jesus' life? What if he had given in?

5. Suggest several examples that show Jesus was still his same thoughtful, loving, and controlled self even in the midst of persecution.

6. Read John 12:23–36 and report on why we can say that Jesus considered his impending death to be glorious.

7. What does the tearing of the veil recorded in Matthew signify? (See also Hebrews 9:1–12; 10:19–22.)

8. How is the verbal abuse recorded in Matthew 27:39–43 similar to the challenges of modern skeptics? How do you answer such demands and accusations?

9. According to Mark 8:34–38, Romans 6:5–11, and Galatians 2:20, how is the believer to identify with the crucifixion of Jesus?

10. What should it mean to twentieth-century people that Jesus tasted such a cruel, painful death? Do you derive any comfort from the awful rejection Jesus suffered?

11. Explain the deep implications of Jesus' petition for the Father to forgive those who were killing him. What can you do to cultivate such a forgiving spirit? Can you think of anyone right now whom you have not forgiven for wronging you?

12. Determine who in the narrative displays these attitudes toward Jesus: rejection, indifference, loyalty. Why are people indifferent to Jesus today? What can we do about it?

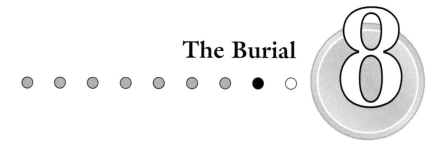

The Burial

Mark 15:38–47

**Joseph took the body, wrapped it in a clean linen
cloth, and placed it in his own new tomb that he had
cut out of the rock.**
Matthew 27:59–60 NIV

Blessed are the poor in spirit.

And Jesus uttered a loud cry, and breathed His last" (Mark
15:37). It was over at last. The misunderstanding, the shame, the
humiliation, the injustice, the pain, the separation—all the horror
of the past twelve hours mercifully came to an end as Jesus expired
on the cross.

Another day's work was done for the Roman soldiers. There was
a great sense of relief for the Jewish leaders who could now prepare
for Passover. Quietness shrouded Golgotha. Only a few sad, confused
folks, mostly women, lingered at the site of history's cruelest crime.

This is not to say that time stood still and events ceased altogether, but the setting and characters changed. After Jesus "yielded

up His Spirit" (Matt. 27:50), the veil in the temple was torn; an earthquake shook the ground; rocks were split; tombs were opened; bodies of dead saints were raised; a centurion became a believer; and a member of the Sanhedrin claimed the body of Jesus, wrapped it in linen, and laid him in a hewn tomb. Another member of the Sanhedrin brought a hundred pounds of spices to assist in preserving the body. A huge rock was rolled over the entrance to the tomb.

These were the postcrucifixion events that occurred on earth, and they present some interesting before-and-after scenes that we will look at carefully.

> **What a great reunion it was!**
> **Think of the joy in heaven.**
> **The Father and Son were reunited.**

Before doing that, however, we need a break from the morose details that have claimed our attention for the past few chapters. Let us look at the triumphal entry. Usually *triumphal entry* describes the Palm Sunday parade when Jesus rode into Jerusalem on the back of a donkey and was hailed as the Messiah. The real triumphal entry, however, was a reentry into heaven as Christ finished his earthly work on the cross and said, "Father, into your hands I commit my spirit" (Luke 23:46 NIV). Although in two days Jesus would be walking through Galilee in his resurrected body, during the hours of his death Jesus made a triumphal entry into the presence of his Father, having been completely obedient to the most important assignment anyone has ever been given. His prayer was being answered: "I have brought you glory on earth by completing the work you gave me to do. And now, Father, glorify me in your presence with the glory I had with you before the world began" (John 17:4–5 NIV).

While Scripture tells very little about the days between the crucifixion and resurrection, perhaps we can pull back the curtain a bit to see what occurred. What a great reunion it was! Think of the joy in heaven. The Father and Son were reunited. Earlier we saw that the Trinity was dissolved as Jesus hung on the cross, the Father having turned his back. The mission was accomplished. No longer would there be any danger that Satan or his agents would derail Jesus from his purpose. Heaven was celebrating. Earth's greatest celebrations, such as the joy of the completed mission of the first astronauts on the moon, pale in comparison to this moment. The enemy was defeated. The seed of the woman had now crushed the head of the serpent (Gen. 3:15). All religious red tape had been cut. All the Old Testament types were fulfilled as Jesus made the Jewish sacrificial system obsolete. He was the last Lamb to be sacrificed. He became the eternal Priest, now representing all of God's people. He won direct access into the heavenlies for us.

Before and After

A whole new day was dawning. To better appreciate this, look at the before-and-after events in this passage. Look at both sides of the cross. What a privilege to be able to do that—to see before and after the cross. Think of the great people of God who never had this privilege. Hebrews 11 lists God's faith hall of fame and declares, "All these people were still living by faith when they died. They did not receive the things promised; they only saw them and welcomed them from a distance" (Heb. 11:13 NIV).

Before-and-after scenes are common to us. On a television commercial a grey-haired man uses a special formula; in the next frame he looks fifteen years younger with just slightly greying hair. A housewife with rough red hands uses a gentle dish-washing liquid. In the next frame her soft smooth hands look as youthful as her daughter's. A young executive flounders in his business until he starts reading the *Wall Street Journal,* which turns him into a prosperous tycoon. Before-and-after scenes are quite familiar to us.

Darkness to Light

The greatest before-and-after scene occurred on that first Good Friday. Before Jesus died the world was plunged into darkness. Afterward the glory of the Holy of Holies in the temple was blazing for all to see. Darkness was transcended by the disclosure of God's glory. Darkness fell over the whole land from the sixth hour until the ninth hour (Mark 15:33). From noon until 3 P.M. God turned out the

> *Now for three hours—physical darkness.*
> *And for three days—spiritual darkness,*
> *the low point of all religious history.*

lights on the world. Jesus had earlier said, "As long as I am in the world I am the light of the world. Night is coming when no one can work" (John 9:4–5, author's paraphrase). The night had now come at high noon, and God was saying, "Here is the true condition of the world spiritually."

Prior to Jesus there was a ray of light as God had revealed himself through prophets and other people of Israel. When Jesus came, the ray became a floodlight. Now for three hours—physical darkness. And for three days—spiritual darkness, the low point of all religious history.

In just a few hours, the Jews would celebrate a meaningless Passover since, now that the blood of the Lamb of God had been spilled, the blood of the temple lambs meant nothing. But this darkness is also a picture of the spiritual condition of those without Christ.

After Christ's death, God revealed a new light to Israel. One that had only been seen once a year by one high priest, namely the *shekinah* glory that filled the Holy of Holies in the temple. A six-inch-thick veil hung as a partition in the temple to separate the Holy Place from the Holy of Holies. When Jesus died, that veil was torn from top to bottom, and for the first time since its construction the Holy of Holies saw the light of day—or more accurately, the world was able to see the light of the Holy of Holies. Hebrews 9 gives us the best explanation of what actually happened when the veil was torn.

> And behind the second veil, there was a tabernacle which is called the Holy of Holies, . . . and above it were the cherubim of glory overshadowing the mercy seat; . . . the priests are continually entering the outer tabernacle, performing the divine worship, but into the second only the high priest enters, once a year, . . . The Holy Spirit is signifying this, that the way into the holy place has not yet been disclosed, while the outer tabernacle is still standing.
>
> Hebrews 9:3, 5–8

Hebrews also suggests that the tearing of the veil in Jerusalem was merely the outward manifestation of Christ's entry into heaven. "For Christ did not enter a holy place made with hands, a mere copy of the true one, but into heaven itself, now to appear in the presence of God for us" (Heb. 9:24).

The symbolism of the veil being torn is twofold. First, no longer is direct access to God available only once a year through the high priest. As Jesus' spirit was torn from his body, the veil was torn to give us access to God. God, like a loving Father, threw open the door and invited us to join him.

Secondly, the veil was torn from top to bottom to show the direction by which true religion must come. Grace goes from top to bottom. Works go from bottom to top. Religion is man's attempt to tear the veil by his own efforts from bottom to top.

While the sanctuary was exposed, another enlightenment occurred. Mark 15:39 indicates that the Roman centurion who was guarding the proceedings saw the way Jesus died. He said, "Truly this man was the Son of God!" Some Bible scholars debate whether the centurion said, *the* Son or *a* Son. The Greek article is indefinite and the argument is fruitless. The argument also misses the point that here was a hard-nosed sergeant major who had seen many a man die but never one like this. The soldier's statement is the second focal point of Mark's Gospel. The first focal point is Peter's statement in Mark 8:29, "Thou art the Christ." First the Jews received enlightenment by God regarding the identity of Jesus. Now a Gentile receives enlightenment as he declares the Sonship of Jesus. Jew and Gentile were drawn to Jesus, "And I, if I be lifted up from the earth, will draw all men to Myself" (John 12:32). Jews and Gentiles conspired to hang him on a cross; now both Jews and Gentiles were drawn to him.

What melted the heart of this soldier? Was it the mysteriousness of the darkness, the courage of Christ, the forgiving spirit of Jesus? We do not know, but he was probably the first genuine Gentile Christian convert.

Abandonment to Attention

Another before-and-after scene is evident in the abandonment of Jesus before his death and the attention shown to him after his death.

At the ninth hour Jesus cried out, *"Eloi, Eloi, lama sabachthani?"* translated, "My God, my God, why have you forsaken me?" (Mark 15:34 NIV). These words are the opening lines of Psalm 22, the most messianic of Psalms. Obviously at that moment Jesus felt very much alone—abandoned even by his Father.

Sometimes we use the phrase *godforsaken* to refer to a lonely, desolate place. Scripture teaches us, however, that no place that God created is godforsaken. David said that if he descended into Hades, God would be even there. The only place ever on God's creation

> ### The cross is God's statement about how seriously he takes sin.

that has been godforsaken was at the cross as our Lord Jesus Christ hung on it. God's abandonment of Jesus was complete because God must turn his back on sin, and Jesus had been made sin for us. We have already seen that by being hung on a tree he was under God's curse.

The cross is God's statement about how seriously he takes sin. Anyone who does not understand why Jesus had to die does not understand God's holiness and justice. Sin had to be judged; therefore, the sins were placed on Jesus, and God turned his back. No person ever alive, regardless of how far he or she has strayed from God, has ever experienced such total abandonment. The Bible does not tell us a great deal about hell, but one thing we are led to believe is that hell is the absence of God. In that sense, Jesus descended into hell, as the creed says, when God abandoned him.

On the other side of the cross we see affectionate attention being given to the dead body of Jesus. Most faithful to Jesus at this time were a few women who followed and served him in Galilee. They were there to mourn the one they loved. They were there to ensure that his abused body received respectful attention. They were there because the Father intended all along for them to be the first to experience the resurrection. According to Matthew, even after the body of Jesus was buried, Mary Magdalene and the other Mary remained sitting opposite the grave (Matt. 27:61). Little were they interested in the Passover celebration that had now claimed the attention of everyone else in Jerusalem. Their Lamb had been slaughtered and it was not a time for joy.

Damnation to Salvation

A third before-and-after scene shows damnation turning into salvation. When Jesus cried out, "My God, my God, why have you forsaken me?" the world heard the most anguished cry ever. While the abuse from Jews and Romans and being abandoned by his friends deeply hurt Jesus, and while the pain of the torturous death on the cross was unbearable, the most mortal blow was struck by God the Father who laid on Jesus all the sins of the world. But it was not just the body of Jesus that died. With him God put to death the power of sin and the power of death. That is why Paul could tell the Corinthian believers, "'Death is swallowed up in victory. O death, where is your victory? O death, where is your sting?' The sting of death is sin, and the power of sin is the law; but thanks be to God, who gives us the victory through our Lord Jesus Christ" (1 Cor. 15:54–57).

The damnation of Jesus on the cross resulted in salvation for others after the cross. Joseph of Arimathea was a prominent member of the Sanhedrin. No doubt he was there as Jesus stood before Caiaphas. Even though he did not consent to the death sentence, he did not publicly object. Why didn't he stand up for Jesus? We do not know. Having watched Jesus die, however, Joseph gathered up his courage. He had been attracted to the life of Jesus; now he had been converted by his death. Perhaps in remorse over his own role in this unjust execution, Joseph determined that he would honor Jesus in his death. Because Joseph was not a relative of Jesus, he had to get consent from Pilate to take the dead body. Technically, because Jesus was convicted of treason, he was not allowed a proper burial, but Pilate, knowing the Jews' motives and Jesus' innocence, allowed Joseph to extend this act of kindness.

When Joseph approached him, Pilate was surprised that Jesus was already dead. The thieves crucified on both sides of Jesus were not yet dead, so according to John's Gospel, the soldiers broke the legs of the two thieves. But seeing that Jesus was already dead, they

> **No doubt through their tears Joseph and Nicodemus expressed their grief over the execution of the most wonderful man they had ever met.**

pierced his side with a spear, "and immediately there came out blood and water" (John 19:34). Pilate, not quite believing that Jesus was dead and wanting to make sure, sent a seasoned centurion to ascertain his death before giving the body to Joseph.

Another member of the Sanhedrin, Nicodemus, who had earlier visited Jesus at night (John 3), came to help Joseph wrap the body in spices and in the linen wrappings before burial. No doubt through their tears Joseph and Nicodemus expressed their grief over the execution of the most wonderful man they had ever met. Up to this point Joseph and Nicodemus were like a great many cultural Christians. Not until thoroughly grappling with the crucifixion can one truly be converted. As Jesus was being separated from God, Joseph was being drawn to him. As Jesus was taking on the damnation of sin, Joseph was being saved from sin.

Blessed Are the Poor in Spirit

Until now we have not identified a beatitude that exemplifies Jesus during the burial episode. Without looking too hard, however, we see that here Jesus was poor in spirit. Jesus did not own anything when he died. And even though he knew he would die, he was unable to make preparation for his own body. Like a poor person, his body would simply be left to the elements apart from the mercy of someone like Joseph. Isaiah 53:9 says,

> His grave was assigned with wicked men,
> Yet He was with a rich man in His death,
> Because He had done no violence,
> Nor was there any deceit in His mouth.

Many have conjectured about why Jesus wept at Lazarus's grave. One possibility, not often offered, is that Jesus, seeing the grave, was overwhelmed by his own impending death. He knew his friend Lazarus had been tenderly cared for and put to rest in his own tomb. The Son of Man not only had nowhere to lay his head, but as one who lived in poverty, he had no place for his dead body.

To be poor in spirit is to have certain attitudes toward life that usually describe the economically depressed, namely, dependence rather than self-sufficiency; social humility rather than elitism and snobbery; frugality rather than indulgence and luxury; and character transparency rather than pseudosophistication.

No one has ever exemplified this beatitude better than Jesus,

> Because He poured out Himself to death,
> And was numbered with the transgressors,
> Yet He Himself bore the sin of many,
> And interceded for the transgressors.
>
> Isaiah 53:12

Group Study

Read Mark 15:38–47 and John 19:31–42.

1. What symbolism do you see in the flowing blood and water from the side of Jesus?
2. Is the saving significance to be found in Jesus' dying or his subsequent bleeding?
3. Drawing from all the Gospel accounts, who verified the death of Jesus?
4. What is the theological significance of John 19:36–37? Consider Exodus 12:46, Numbers 9:12, Isaiah 53:5, Zechariah 12:10, and Revelation 1:7.
5. From the description in all four Gospels, put together a verbal character sketch of Joseph of Arimathea.
6. Name several things that Nicodemus and Joseph of Arimathea had in common. What thoughts and emotions must they have had as they went about their unpleasant undertaking?
7. Do you think Nicodemus and Joseph knew each other's feelings for Jesus before they met at the cross? If not, why not?

If so, why didn't they have courage to stand together for Jesus at the trial?

8. Of what were Joseph of Arimathea and Nicodemus fearful so that they kept their discipleship secret? What fears inhibit modern believers from declaring love for Jesus publicly?

9. Besides using a borrowed grace, what indications in Passion Week demonstrate that Jesus was poor in spirit?

10. What are some of the motives that inspire people to give to the Lord's cause today? How do you think God responds to either selfish or calculated giving?

11. What is significant about the fact that Jesus occupied a tomb that had never been used? If you consider your heart to be his present lodging place, does he occupy it alone, or must he compete with other inhabitants?

12. Many efforts have been made to explain away the empty tomb—the so-called "swoon theory," the wrong tomb, and a stolen corpse are a few. What do these words suggest, and how does the evidence in Matthew and Mark discredit these theories?

The Resurrection

● ● ● ● ● ● ● ● ●

Mark 16:1–13

"Don't be alarmed," he said. "You are looking for
Jesus the Nazarene, who was crucified. He has risen!
He is not here. See the place where they laid him."
Mark 16:6 NIV

. . . for theirs is the kingdom of heaven.
. . . for they will be comforted.
. . . for they will inherit the earth.
. . . for they will be filled.
. . . for they will be shown mercy.
. . . for they will see God.
. . . for they will be called the sons of God.
. . . for theirs is the kingdom of God.

The passion of Jesus is over. What a great story it has been.
Eight episodes where Jesus majestically demonstrated the graces of
God that he taught his disciples and that we call the beatitudes.

Mary of Bethany created a stir that resulted in strife among the Lord's people by anointing him with an extravagant ointment. Jesus was the *peacemaker* who brought his people back together to focus on eternal truths.

In the upper room, the disciples gathered with Jesus to eat the Passover feast. The story took on greater meaning as Jesus said that the bread and wine symbolized his body and blood. Although he could foresee the terror of the cross, he earnestly desired to eat this meal; thus demonstrating his *hunger and thirst for righteousness*— God's saving activity.

Wanting a time of prayerful preparation prior to the ordeal he would endure, Jesus took his disciples to the Garden of Gethsemane. There he entered the valley of the shadow of death as the horror of sin overwhelmed him. In deep grief and anguish Jesus submitted fully to the Father and exhibited the right spirit as he *mourned* the damning effects of sin.

Over six hundred soldiers and Jewish officers interrupted the tranquility of the garden. As Jesus was being arrested, his disciples came to his defense. Jesus reminded them that he could call twelve legions of angels to assist him if that were his goal. By his restraint Jesus demonstrated the blessed quality of being *merciful.*

Through several official, unofficial, and illegal trials before the Jews, Jesus remained calm and silent. His only reply to the badgering and false testimony was to admit that he was the Christ, the Son of the Blessed One. Knowing full well that this would be a condemning statement, Jesus still uttered it, demonstrating that he was *pure in heart.*

Similarly, in the Roman trial, Jesus remained passive to the verbal and physical abuse. As the Roman soldiers mocked him and mercilessly pummeled his body, Jesus remained like a sheep before its shearers, quiet, gentle, and *meek.*

The crucifixion brought the greatest physical suffering to Jesus. A crown of thorns, spikes through his wrists and ankles, a lacerated back against the rough tree—were just the most obvious sources of pain. Jesus, by enduring this mistreatment and the cruel verbal abuse of bystanders, personified another beatitude: *persecuted because of righteousness.*

The final indignity was having to be buried in a borrowed tomb.

While the generosity of Joseph of Arimathea is exemplary, the abject poverty of the Son of Man is also evident. In his death he identified with the *poor in spirit.*

By perfectly exemplifying all eight beatitudes during even the stress-filled Passion Week, Jesus made himself the most "blessed" man. You might think, if that's blessing, I'd just as soon pass. But

> ### *Resurrection is not an epilogue or a postscript. The resurrection of Jesus is the centerpiece of all history.*

look at the promises of the beatitudes. The middle six offer deferred blessing—"for they will . . ." Jesus knew that investing his life according to the beatitudes would fit him for a future of blessing. The other two beatitudes promise the presence of the kingdom now, a blessing so abundant that those enjoying it gladly endure the sacrifices of living as Jesus taught.

Beyond the Tomb

The passion story is filled with intrigue, emotion, and heroism. By itself, the story is the most poignant moment of history. But thank God for Matthew 28, Mark 16, Luke 24, and John 20. All four Gospel writers went beyond the tomb. Death is not the final chapter. Resurrection is not an epilogue or a postscript. The resurrection of Jesus is the centerpiece of all history, the reason the evangelists reported the Passion Week, and the final convincing proof that Jesus is the Messiah.

Without the resurrection of Jesus, there is no hope beyond this life, no eternal life, no salvation, no meaning to history, and no reason to be religious. The resurrection of Jesus is either true or false. He either rose from the tomb or he did not. He either is now alive or he is not. There is no middle ground, no compromise, no third possibility. Let us not fool ourselves into thinking that the resurrection records are fanciful bits of fiction created by grief-stricken men or conniving, deceiving charlatans. Let us not glory in the moral example of Jesus. Let us not try to separate the Jesus of history from the

Christ of faith. Without resurrection, the crucifixion is meaningless and might just as well be forgotten.

Let us travel the road of honesty that leads us either to deny altogether the historical trustworthiness of the Gospels from beginning to end, in which case Christianity is a hoax, or to believe the literal integrity of the Gospel records as they present the resurrection of Jesus Christ.

As we examine the resurrection records we find no lack of evidence. On the contrary, the variety and complexity of the evidence seem baffling at first. Philosophers have for centuries divided truth into two kinds: that which may be known by *a priori* reasoning and that which is verifiable by *a posteriori* evidence. *A priori* knowledge is obtainable by deductive reasoning—if *a* equals *b*, and *b* equals *c*, then *a* must equal *c*. *A posteriori* knowledge comes from empirical facts that are commonly considered in two categories: scientific and historical. Scientific empirical facts occur in the presence of those reporting on them and are by nature repeatable. An example of this is that helium is lighter than air. Every time a balloon is filled with helium the balloon rises. We can repeat this experiment any time we choose. Historical knowledge comes from those events that were reported to have occurred, were observed in history, and by nature are not repeatable events. For example, George Washington and his soldiers crossed the Delaware River in 1776. We know this, not by rational deduction nor by scientific experimentation, but by the report of historical witnesses. We may choose to believe or not believe in the reliability of the witnesses. We may not, however, say that the event did not occur simply because it is not repeatable in our day. George Washington is dead. The year 1776 will never again occur.

The resurrection of Jesus cannot be known through rational deduction or scientific experimentation. Most skeptics choose not to believe the reality of the resurrection because they come with an *a priori* assumption that dead people do not rise. They also maintain that resurrection is not empirically verifiable and, because there seem to be no records of other people who have risen from the dead, they conclude that the resurrection reports must be false.

We are left then with a decision regarding the historical trustworthiness of people who lived in the first century. We will look at their claims later.

Dead . . . Buried . . . Gone

As we examine historical evidence, three empirical truths are evident to all observers: Jesus was dead, Jesus was buried, and the tomb was empty on Sunday morning.

First, Jesus was dead. Jesus was crucified. He died within six hours. Soldiers who had seen many crucifixions testified to his death. One soldier shoved a spear through Jesus' side out of which flowed blood

> *Three empirical facts—a dead body, a burial, and an empty tomb—were all verified in Jerusalem during the first century.*

and water, medical evidence that death had occurred. Had he been alive, blood would have spouted with each heartbeat; instead, clotted blood separated from watery serum was evidence of massive clotting, an exceptionally strong medical proof of death. John, who reported these events, could never have realized their significance to a pathologist.

Second, Jesus was buried. Joseph of Arimathea, who certainly never expected Jesus to rise, sought permission from Pilate to bury the body. Nicodemus brought a mixture of myrrh and aloes that weighed about a hundred pounds, according to John's Gospel, to assist with the burial. The two men wound strips of linen tightly around the corpse and lifted Jesus into a shelflike chamber and rolled a heavy stone over the entrance.

In a highly acclaimed book, *The Passover Plot* by Hugh Schonfield, skeptics were treated to an argument that suggested that Jesus never really died. Supposedly, in the cool of the tomb, Jesus' strength revived, he somehow removed the stone, crept out, and persuaded his gullible disciples that he had risen from the dead. Schonfield's argument somehow neglects the deadly character of the wounds, the careful examination of the experienced soldiers, the spear thrust into Jesus' side, the constricting grave clothes, the crushing weight of spices, the lack of human help, the unlikelihood of reviving in a cold damp tomb, and the heavy rock that sealed the tomb. Schon-

> **The challenge facing any honest seeker is to weigh the alternatives. Why was the tomb empty?**

field also neglects the psychological impossibility of someone's creeping out from a tomb half-dead, needing bandaging, strengthening, and care, and subsequently dying in obscurity, giving the impression that he was the Lord of life and conqueror of death.[1]

The third empirical fact was the empty tomb on Sunday morning. Matthew, Mark, Luke, John, Peter, Mary Magdalene, and Mary, the mother of Jesus specifically attest to the empty tomb. Undoubtedly scores of others—Jews, Romans, and disciples—hurried to the tomb that first day. The body was gone. About that there can be no doubt. Three empirical facts—a dead body, a burial, and an empty tomb—were all verified by humans in Jerusalem during the first century.

The challenge facing any honest seeker is to weigh the alternatives. Why was the tomb empty? All hangs on this question: What are the possibilities? Three seem to be plausible—enemies took the body; friends took the body; God raised up Jesus.

Neither Enemies nor Friends

Why would the enemies of Jesus steal the body, and which enemies would do it? The Jewish leaders at last had Jesus where they wanted him—dead and buried. They knew he had claimed that he would rise from the dead. And Matthew's Gospel tells us,

> Now on the next day, which is the one after the preparation, the chief priests and the Pharisees gathered together with Pilate, and said, "Sir, we remember that when He was still alive that deceiver said, 'After three days I am to rise again.' Therefore, give orders for the grave to be made secure until the third day, lest the disciples come and steal Him away and say to the people, 'He is risen from the dead,' and the last deception will be worse than the first." Pilate said to them, "You have a guard; go, make it as secure as you know how." And they went and made the grave secure, and along with the guard they set a seal on the stone.
>
> Matthew 27:62–66

Clearly it was in the interest of the Jews for Jesus to remain dead and buried. Had they moved his body, when reports of his resurrection began to circulate, they easily could have produced the corpse and stopped all the rumors.

The only other enemies of Jesus would have been the Romans. No one yet has suggested a plausible motive for them to have moved the body. The passage cited above indicates that Pilate was fully cooperative with the Jews in wanting to keep Jesus buried. Likewise, had the Romans moved the body of Jesus, once claims about a resurrection began circulating, the Romans could easily have produced the corpse.

More plausible is the idea that the friends of Jesus took the body. That, in fact, is exactly what the Jewish leaders circulated as an explanation. After the guards, who had been traumatized by the appearance of angels (Matt. 28:4), came to their senses and reported the events of the resurrection, the chief priests assembled with the elders and came up with a scheme. Giving a large sum of money to the soldiers, they said,

> "You are to say, 'His disciples came by night and stole Him away while we were asleep.' And if this should come to the governor's ears, we will win him over and keep you out of trouble." And they took the money and did as they had been instructed; and this story was widely spread among the Jews, and is to this day.
>
> Matthew 28:13–15

Several considerations render this alternative implausible. First, the disciples could not have stolen the body. Do not fail to observe that the soldiers who were posted on guard were not Roman soldiers. Pilate told the Jewish leaders to have their own guards keep watch over the tomb. Roman guards might have been bribed, but Jewish guards certainly would not have been susceptible to a bribe.

They had no thought of carrying on the cause of one who led them on a three-year wild-goose chase.

Therefore, the Jewish leaders concocted the lame story about the guards falling asleep.

Secondly, even if the disciples could have stolen the body, they would not have done so. They were utterly disheartened men, anxious only to run, hide, and forget the whole affair. They had no thought of carrying on the cause of one who led them on a three-year wild-goose chase. Although Jesus had predicted his resurrection, the disciples never really embraced the idea. They surely did not expect one so brutally murdered to come back from the dead. The Gospel accounts ring true as they describe each witness of the resurrection being totally surprised.

But even if we could credit eleven men and a few women with such cunning at their moment of greatest grief, what about the sequel? We find them joyfully proclaiming the resurrection of Jesus, preaching it with conviction so convincingly that thousands of people in Jerusalem become believers. How would they have staged the subsequent miracles? How would they have explained the astonishing events we find in Acts 2 where over three thousand people believed?

Beyond that, however, ten of the eleven disciples endured prison, torture, and various forms of brutal execution because of their belief and proclamation that Jesus was alive. Maurice Goguel wrote, "Men might indeed be willing to die for a passionately held illusion but not for a piece of flagrant deception."[2]

The third possible explanation for the empty tomb is that God raised up Jesus, the Gospel accounts are accurate, and the eyewitness account of the disciples is true. Peter, who of all people had most reason to be ashamed and glad that the events were over, is found to be boldly challenging the Jewish leaders.

> Men of Israel, listen to these words: Jesus the Nazarene, a man attested to you by God with miracles and wonders and signs which God performed through Him in your midst, just as you yourselves know—this Man, delivered up by the predetermined plan and foreknowledge of God, you nailed to a cross by the hands of godless men and put Him to death. And God raised Him up again, putting an end to the agony of death, since it was impossible for Him to be held in its power.
>
> Acts 2:22–24

> ### *Faith without facts is mere fantasy.*
> ### *The facts are our friends.*

He went on to say, "This Jesus God raised up again, to which we are all witnesses" (Acts 2:32).

Peter's powerful message gave birth to another historically incontrovertible, empirical evidence of the truth of Jesus' resurrection: A host of believers, from then on called the Christian church, which to this day continues as testimony to the credibility of these early witnesses.

Friendly Facts

In the nineteenth century a new brand of philosophy that we now call existentialism surfaced in the writings of a devout Christian Dane, Søren Kierkegaard. Because the European state churches allowed the objectivity of doctrinal truth to chill devotional fervor, Kierkegaard emphasized the importance of subjective faith for Christian belief. In retrospect, we find that he allowed the pendulum to swing too far by denigrating the objective and historical elements that form the basis for faith. Unfortunately, in the decades that followed, men less devout than he, and certainly not Christian, took Kierkegaard's premises to their logical conclusions. Existential thinking, rather than being a fertilizer for the ground of faith, has proven to be poison. Faith without facts is mere fantasy. The facts are our friends. Therefore, our pursuing further historical clues will be helpful.

The Scriptures report a number of postcrucifixion appearances by Jesus to various individuals. Mary of Magdala and Mary the mother of Jesus were the first to see the resurrected Jesus. A skeptic might say, "Well, this is not very impressive. Here are emotional women dazed with bereavement, very susceptible to fantasizing." A closer look indicates that the very vulnerability of the story argues for its truth. Had the Gospel writers intended to invent the story to foster a myth, they certainly would not have begun with these two women. In the first century, the witness of women, especially distraught women, would not have been very impressive. If the disciples were trying to build a case based on fiction, the witness of women was a weak beginning point.

Another appearance was experienced by two unknown disciples who were traveling to Emmaus from Jerusalem. They were thoroughly discouraged about the crucifixion events and certainly never expected to encounter Jesus again. Luke 24 tells about the marvelous visitation of Jesus to them.

Jesus then appeared to ten of the original disciples, and his very presence startled them. They certainly were not expecting to see him; clearly his appearance was not a psychological fantasy due to wish fulfillment. One of the original disciples, Thomas, was not present during that appearance and held to his skepticism against the strong assurances of the other ten that they had seen Jesus. Thomas demanded empirical proof. We can be grateful for him because he expressed the spirit of the twentieth century. On a subsequent gathering of the disciples Jesus appeared and specifically fulfilled Thomas's wish by inviting him to examine the wounds (John 20:24–27).

Jesus' appearances to his disciples are sometimes minimized as evidence by modern skeptics. They tend to forget that these men were not simpletons. The assumption is that these poor, primitive men did not have our standards of critical judgment. The truth is, they no more expected to see a dead man walking around than we would. They were just as incredulous, just as hesitant, just as skeptical. There were initial doubts about every appearance. The Scriptures indicate that during a period of forty days Jesus appeared at least twenty times to various individuals and groups. Paul told the Corinthians that more than five hundred people saw the resurrected Jesus (1 Cor. 15:6).

Nevertheless, it is legitimate to ask whether these appearances were fabricated by the early Christians. Several ideas suggest that these were not fabrications. We have already seen that men do not suffer and die for a practical joke that they perpetrate and know to be a hoax. Another factor is the lack of uniformity in the appearances. Were the stories made up, we would expect uniformity. Furthermore, if the appearances were fabricated, they would have included an eyewitness to the actual resurrection. It would have been reported that someone was on the scene when the angels came and rolled

> **The truth is, they no more expected to see a dead man walking around than we would.**

back the stone. Also the strange composition of a resurrected body would have been difficult to invent, modern science-fiction writers notwithstanding. Is it likely that a first-century writer would have invented a body that seemed to be neither completely material nor completely spiritual? Jesus could walk through a door, but he also could eat fish. It is thus quite unlikely that the strange appearances of Jesus were fabricated stories.

Some have suggested that these appearances were hallucinations. More careful consideration works against that idea. A wide variety of temperament types saw the resurrected Jesus, whereas hallucinations generally attend certain particular personalities and are often the result of wish fulfillment. We have already seen how unlikely it is that anyone expected to see Jesus alive again. Furthermore, if these were hallucinations, they lasted for forty days and then abruptly ended. And finally, there seems to be no uniform locale or time to these alleged hallucinations.

What then fits the facts regarding these strange appearances of the resurrected Jesus? Besides the empty tomb and the resurrection appearances, any credible explanation must make room for the amazing change that occurred in the disciples. They became so convinced that Jesus was alive that they fearlessly proclaimed his resurrection even to the Jewish authorities who had executed Jesus. We have seen that prior to the crucifixion the disciples were a cowering bunch who quickly disbanded. No mere psychological gimmick could have so altered the mentality and personality of all these men. It would be incredible to think that these eleven men could have gone back to their homes and fishing, only to return six weeks later to admonish the clergy about their complicity in the murder of a man that God raised to life. And, instead of being laughed into silence by the crowd, they won the crowd over.

We must understand that first-century cosmology makes no more allowance for resurrection than does twentieth-century science. In fact, twentieth-century science, despite enormous advances in knowledge and discovery, still does not have the last word regarding all occurrences and events in the world. A contemporary research scientist, Dr. Roger Pilkington, wrote,

> If matter is no more than an arrangement of energy, then it is perfectly conceivable that where the sheer essence of the whole creation was poured into human form, the body could disassociate into sheer energy and re-distill, as it were, outside the tomb in a state which on the average was more energy than matter, but definitely material enough to have some shape and substance.[3]

True science, which does not begin with unprovable assertions regarding the impossibility of metaphysics, must humbly allow for facts and events that are outside the parameters of its discoveries and theorems.

Truly the resurrection of Jesus is not an experiment that can be repeated. But historical evidence and the mystery of the relationship between energy and matter cited by Dr. Pilkington argue for the plausibility of the resurrection.

Besides Jesus' strange appearances after his crucifixion, another clue to the truth of the resurrection is Sunday. Never before had Sunday been a day of worship. The Sabbath, our Saturday, ended at sundown, and Sunday was merely the first day of the week—a day for normal work and commerce. Soon after the crucifixion, however, a whole band of heretofore orthodox Jews were found to be worshipping on Sunday. The explanation, of course, is that the first day of the week was the resurrection day—a logical time for Christians to worship Christ and celebrate the special meal he had given them.

Another resurrection evidence is baptism. Until this time, baptism was primarily for Gentiles, who converted to Judaism, or for others being inducted into one of the mystery cults. Circumcision was the normal initiatory rite for Jews. After the crucifixion, baptism became the new initiation rite for all believers, who were told to repent of their sins, believe in the risen Lord, and be baptized for acceptance with God in the name of Jesus.

Holy Communion, likewise, was a new feature within Judaism. Let's remember that for quite some time all Christians were Jewish people who had no intention of starting a new religion. They were merely working out within Judaism the ramifications of the Lord's teaching and his resurrection. Communion was not a cult feast in honor of a dead hero, but a rendezvous with the living Jesus. They were aware of his presence in the breaking of the bread, even though it was a mystical experience. They claimed to meet him in the sacrament, celebrating his death but conscious of his risen presence. The ritual ended with a eucharistic prayer uttered in Aramaic, *Maranatha,* meaning *Our Lord, come!* (1 Cor. 16:22). How could that have been the yearning of these early Christians unless they truly believed that Jesus rose from the dead?

I am not suggesting that belief in the resurrection is easy or even logical. But in the face of all the evidence—the certified death of Jesus, his burial, the empty tomb, the changed lives of the disciples, the many postcrucifixion appearances to credible witnesses, the new day of worship, the new sacraments, the fulfillment of Scripture (which we have not explored carefully)—difficult though it may be to believe, any alternative suggestion is even harder to believe. The

> **The communion was not a cult feast in honor of a dead hero, but a rendezvous with the living Jesus.**

evidence points unmistakably to the fact that on the third day Jesus rose from the dead. That is why leading Jewish intellectuals of the first century, people like Paul of Tarsus and Roman politicians like Sergius Paulus, governor of Cyprus, became committed followers of Jesus Christ. That is also why Lord Darling, former Lord Chief Justice of England, came to the same conclusion. At a private dinner party the discussion turned to a certain book that dealt with the idea of resurrection. Lord Darling is said to have stated,

> We as Christians are asked to take a very great deal on trust; the teachings, for example, and the miracles of Jesus. If we had to take all on trust, I for one should be skeptical. The crux of the problem of whether Jesus was or was not what he proclaimed himself to be must surely depend upon the truth or otherwise of the resurrection. On that greatest point we are not merely asked to have faith. In its favor as a living

truth there exists such overwhelming evidence, positive and negative, factual and circumstantial, that no intelligent jury in the world could fail to bring in a verdict that the resurrection story is true.[4]

The lines can be clearly drawn. One either believes Jesus was resurrected and is alive today or believes he was not resurrected and remains dead. If Jesus is not really risen from the dead, then we who believe are the worst fools in the world, happy and hopeful though we may be. If Jesus has risen from the dead, he will return and judge all people. In that case, those who do not believe will be found to be the worst fools in the world.

Thousands of people died on Roman crosses; only One is worshipped today by over a billion people. Hundreds of people have claimed to be a messiah; only One is worshipped today by over a billion people.

Jesus claimed to be the Messiah. He predicted he would rise from the dead. He established a church nearly two thousand years ago and now it is over a billion members strong. Is there any reason not to believe that he will yet again appear even as he said: "I will come again, and receive you to Myself; that where I am, there you may be also" (John 14:3)?

> **Thousands of people died on Roman crosses; only One is worshipped today by over a billion people.**

The passion of our Lord ended during that first Holy Week. But the Easter story goes on. Jesus was crucified, taking our punishment. He was resurrected, guaranteeing our eternal salvation. *Maranatha.*

Group Study

Read Mark 16:1–13 and John 20:1–31.

1. In what sense does John's account have a different emphasis from that of the other Gospel writers'?

2. What evidence in the Gospels suggests that none of the fol-
    lowers of Jesus expected him to be resurrected?
3. How does the account of the grave clothes add to the weight
    of evidence for the resurrection?
4. From what you know in other Scriptures about Mary Mag-
    dalene, Simon Peter, John, and Thomas, conjecture a bit
    about their emotions and attitudes to this astonishing good
    news.
5. How can you be sure the postresurrection appearances of
    Jesus were neither hallucinations nor phantom appearances?
6. John was not the least bit subtle about his evangelistic pur-
    pose (20:31). How do his autobiographical sections in the
    Passion-Week narrative add urgency to his message? (See
    13:23, 25; 18:15; 19:27, 35; 20:8.)
7. Why do you think Jesus appeared first to Mary Magdalene?
    Does this suggest anything about how you can realize his
    presence more readily?
8. Sorrow is turned into joy (John 20:11–16), fear is turned
    into boldness (vv. 19–23), and doubt is turned into belief
    (vv. 24–26) by the encounters with Jesus. What transforma-
    tions have occurred in your life since you encountered
    Christ?
9. Just how important is the resurrection of Jesus to Christian
    faith? Try to support your claims with Scripture.
10. Explain the modern-day importance of Jesus' words in John
    20:29. How are Christians today sometimes like Thomas?
11. What other concern did Jesus have in these appearances
    besides proving that he was alive? (See Matt. 28:19, 29;
    Luke 24:46–47; John 20:21–22.) What motivation does he
    assume will compel them to obey?
12. Conclude by reading and reflecting on Acts 1:3–11.

Notes

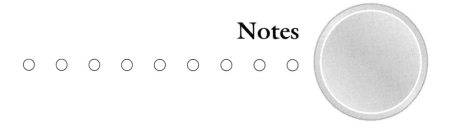

Chapter One: The Anointing

1. For a discussion of this important discourse see chapter 14 of my book, *"Follow Me": The Master's Plan for Men.*
2. Passover is the celebration of the exodus from Egypt. It is held annually on the fourteenth day of Nisan (our April/May months). Normally having a population of fifty thousand, Jerusalem's population swelled to three million during Passover.
3. T. W. Manson, *The Servant Messiah* (London: Cambridge University Press, 1961), 84–85.

Chapter Two: The Last Supper

1. Robert Boyd Munger, *My Heart Christ's Home* (Madison: Inter-Varsity Press, 1954).

Chapter Three: The Garden Prayer

1. Vincent Taylor, *The Gospel According to St. Mark,* 2nd ed. (London: Macmillan Press, 1966), 552.
2. Charles Colson, *The Body* (Dallas: Word, 1992), 128.

Chapter Five: The Jewish Trial and Peter's Denial

1. William Barclay, "The Gospel of Mark" in *The Daily Bible Study* (Philadelphia: Westminster Press, 1954), 371.
2. A. W. Tozer, *Five Vows for Spiritual Power* (Harrisburg, Pa.: Christian Publications, Inc., n.d.).
3. B. F. Wescott, quoted in A. T. Robertson, *Epochs in the Life of Simon Peter* (Grand Rapids: Baker Book House, 1974), 137.

Chapter Six: The Roman Trial

1. Tozer, *Five Vows for Spiritual Power*, 11.
2. Colson, *The Body*, 151.
3. Emile Cailliet, *Pascal: The Emergence of Genius* (New York: Harper & Brothers, 1946), 330.

Chapter Seven: The Crucifixion

1. Max Lucado, *No Wonder They Call Him the Savior* (Portland: Multnomah Press, 1986), 12.
2. Quoted in William Barclay, "The Gospel of Mark," 381.
3. Paul Little, *Know What You Believe* (Wheaton: Scripture Press Publications, Inc., 1970), 92.
4. C. Truman Davis, "The Crucifixion of Jesus," in *Arizona Medicine,* March 1965, 183–87.

Chapter Nine: The Resurrection

1. Quoted in Michael Green, *Man Alive!* (Chicago: InterVarsity Press, 1967), 33–34.
2. Ibid., 41.
3. Ibid., 47.
4. Quoted by Josh McDowell, *Evidence That Demands a Verdict* (Campus Crusade for Christ, 1973), 201.

David E. Schroeder is president of Nyack College. He holds an Ed.D. in religious education and is founder of MasterWorks, an interdenominational organization committed to helping local churches disciple men.